Sailor
for the Wild

Sailor for the Wild
On Maine, Conservation and Boats
Copyright © 2017 by Ben Emory
Seapoint Books + Media LLC
PO Box 21, Brooklin, ME 04616
www.seapointbooks.com

Book design by Claire MacMaster, barefoot art graphic design
Maps by Jane Crosen with Barbara Tedesco
Catspaw dinghy illustration original drawing by Spencer Lincoln;
copyright WoodenBoat

Printed by Printworks Global Ltd, London & Hong Kong
First Edition

ISBN 13: 978-0-9973920-6-7
ISBN 10: 0-9973920-6-7

Sailor
for the Wild

On Maine,
Conservation and Boats

BEN EMORY

Contents

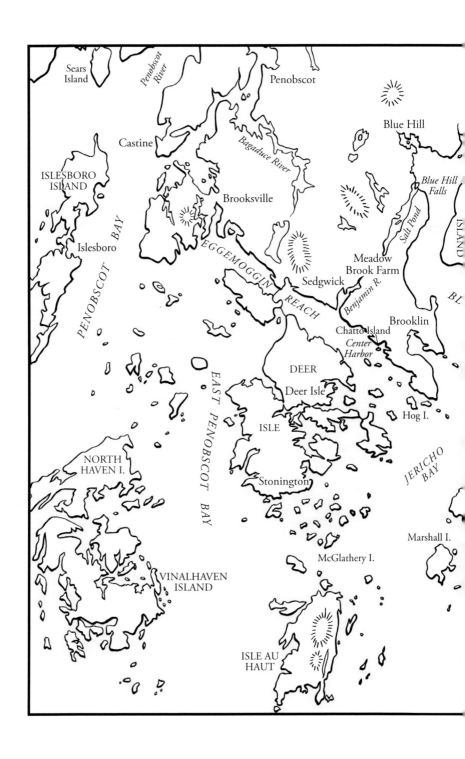

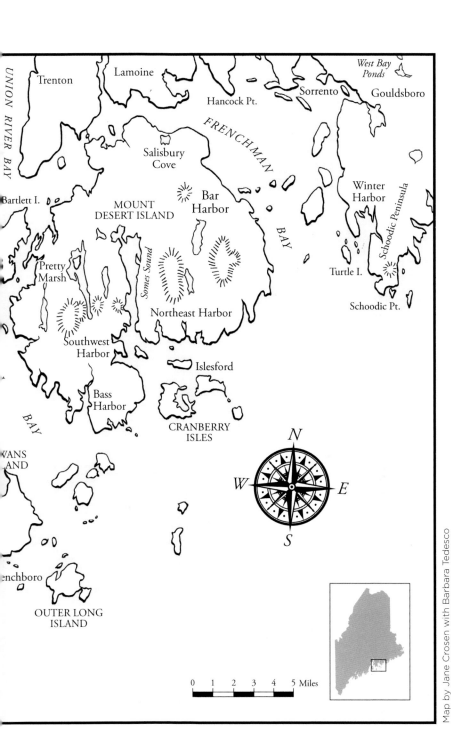

UNION RIVER BAY

Trenton   Lamoine   West Bay
                                      Ponds
              Hancock Pt.   Sorrento   Gouldsboro

                    FRENCHMAN
         Salisbury
         Cove

Bartlett I.   Winter
         MOUNT   Bar   Harbor
         DESERT ISLAND Harbor

                                               Schoodic Peninsula
                                        BAY

Pretty   Turtle I.
Marsh
              Somes Sound   Schoodic Pt.

                    Northeast Harbor

Southwest
Harbor

              Islesford
Bass
Harbor
              CRANBERRY
              ISLES
BAY

VANS
AND
                    N

                W   E

                    S

enchboro

OUTER LONG
ISLAND

0   1   2   3   4   5 Miles

Map by Jane Crosen with Barbara Tedesco

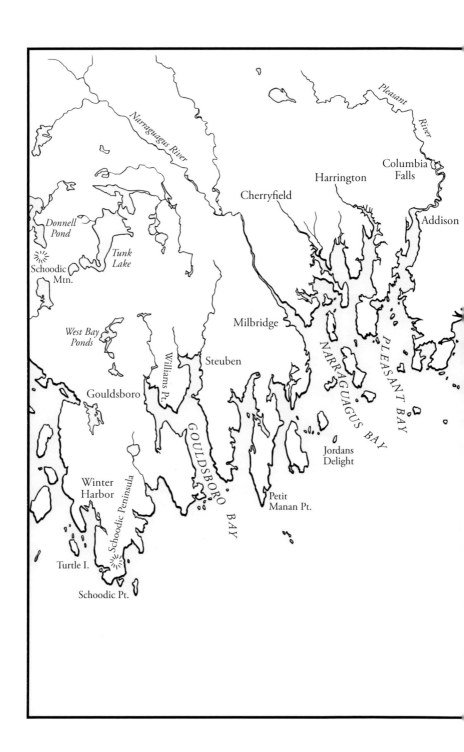

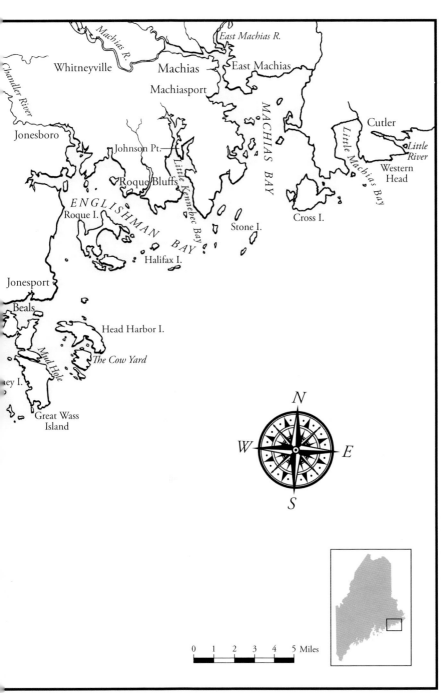

Machias R.

East Machias R.

Whitneyville

Chandler River

Machias

East Machias

Machiasport

Jonesboro

Cutler

Little River

Johnson Pt.

Western Head

MACHIAS BAY

Little Machias Bay

Roque Bluffs

ENGLISHMAN BAY

Little Kennebec Bay

Roque I.

Stone I.

Cross I.

Halifax I.

Jonesport

Beals

Head Harbor I.

Mud Hole

The Cow Yard

ey I.

Great Wass Island

N

W   E

S

0 1 2 3 4 5 Miles

INTRODUCTION

Maine's magnificent coastal landscape and the surrounding ocean have been driving forces of my life. Many choices I have made, for better or worse, trace back to intense devotion to the Maine coast. Because of lifelong exposure to this coastal landscape I developed my addiction to the sport of sailing and strong interest in all things related to the sea. Love for Maine led to wanting to engage in protecting what makes Maine so special and to nearly fifty years working both professionally and as a volunteer in the conservation of land, primarily although not exclusively in Maine. British author Robert MacFarlane in his book *The Old Ways: A Journey on Foot* wrote, "I have always been . . . interested in the relationship between landscape and individual lives, and how the places we inhabit shape the people we are." As I read those words in my study overlooking the upper reaches of Maine's Frenchman Bay, I realized that if anyone has been shaped by a landscape, it is I.

My twin passions of sailing and the sea, on the one hand, and conservation, on the other, have been deeply intertwined. Exploring the Maine coast under sail has taught me about its geography, people, scenery, and wildlife. Through my sailing in Maine and elsewhere I developed contacts with people and learned lessons that made me more effective when I began professional work, initially focused on preserving the scenic and natural qualities of Maine's coastal islands. Over the years, as I have explored and enjoyed the Maine coast in a wide variety of sailing and rowing vessels, I have gained knowledge and inspiration on the water that have proved beneficial in my engagement in the conservation of Maine's land resources. In the worlds of both boats and land conservation I have witnessed major changes, truly staggering in retrospect.

My fascination with boats has been both as recreation and as an art form. My fascination with land has been with the host of conservation values that a property may possess, very much including scenic magnificence, nature's own art form. Both forms of art—lovely boats and beautiful landscapes—rejuvenate my soul.

I know that if I had not been exposed from earliest childhood to the natural world as it presents itself on the coast of Maine, I would have been slower to awake to the implications of what humankind and civilization face as environmental changes accelerate on the land, in the air, and in the water. Thinking ahead to the world my grandchildren will inherit, I realize that my own experiences in Maine afloat and ashore are why I so strongly believe in the critical importance of getting all children outdoors. Says another British writer, Michael McCarthy, in *The Moth Snowstorm—Nature and Joy*, "For a young person to fall in love with a place is surely one of life's greatest blessings. . . ." Young people, if they are to grow into adults who will cherish and properly steward this planet that is their home, need to experience nature in enjoyable ways as much as possible. Wherever they live, they must learn to appreciate the natural world in all its facets and have opportunities to fall in love with natural places special to them.

My goals in sharing with readers my twin and interrelated passions are: (1) to entertain—for much over the years has been entertaining; (2) to educate and inspire—because I have been privileged to learn important lessons and to participate in inspiring aspects of both conservation and nautical history; and (3) to add my own tiny contribution to commentary about challenges that Maine and the world face, perhaps especially timely in this era of rapidly mounting environmental and social concerns and massive failures in political leadership. Anecdotes, vignettes, and flavor I stress over comprehensiveness, but some history particulars about which I have written are very much worth recording. Hopefully, readers interested in Maine, the conservation of lands and waters, wherever located, and the pleasure and art of good boats will find time spent with this book rewarding.

1

TWO PASSIONS

My passions colluded to nearly kill me. "Ben, you are in a predicament!" I kept repeating to myself as I failed to banish thoughts of pending hypothermia and perhaps drowning. The northwest wind of a strong Memorial Day cold front howled down Maine's frigid Eggemoggin Reach, blowing the tops off the waves as I perched on the rail of my swamped small sailboat. Would the flotation tanks of this lead-ballasted Cape Cod Bulls Eye keep her afloat indefinitely? Was there any hope of blowing ashore on an island, and if so, what about surviving the cold night ahead? In the grayness of the late afternoon no other boats were visible, and none were likely to be out.

That I was on the water pursuing my never-ending wish to sail as often as possible resulted from failing to understand from the weather forecast heard the previous day that two cold fronts, not one, were to pass over coastal Maine. The second was to be far stronger than the first. After passage of the first I mistakenly believed that we were in a stable weather pattern. When the wind had suddenly shifted from southwest to northwest and quickly tripled in velocity, I had succeeded in scudding downwind to the relative safety of a mooring off the dock of the WoodenBoat School. I could have stayed there and eventually made it to shore, but I deeply reefed the mainsail, cast off, and headed upwind for home, lulled by what turned out to be a very temporary drop in windspeed.

My haste came from an overwhelming, judgment-destroying determination to be home in time for a scheduled telephone call with the owners of a large parcel of eastern Maine land of considerable scenic and recreational importance. They were considering permanently preserving it for public benefit, and we were ready to discuss next steps. I have always loved projects that preserve the natural qualities of Maine and certainly did not want to miss a beat on this one.

The boat and I struggled homeward toward that telephone call, and we seemed to be managing. I was on home waters, which I have sailed for a lifetime. The boat is one in which I have spent countless hours and in which I have much confidence. Perhaps I let down my guard for a minute. All I know is that suddenly the leeward rail was under water and going deeper fast. Even as I jammed the tiller to leeward in a frantic effort to bring the bow into the wind and the boat upright, I knew, sickeningly, that it was too late. Water poured over the rail into the cockpit and into the open area under the foredeck. I was doomed in terms of getting sailing again, for there was no way to bail or pump. The boat was floating at a 45-degree angle with the entire leeward coaming underwater, even after I hauled down the sails.

I have no idea how long I pondered my predicament, alone on Eggemoggin Reach with an outgoing current and nearly invisible from shore. I do not think that it was very long. I never saw the big yawl approaching under power. Suddenly, very close ahead of me she loomed. She steered along my windward side as two strong crew members stood by her lifelines. As she passed inches from my boat, I put my feet on the rail and leapt. Each of my arms was grabbed, and I was hauled over the lifelines—safe and astounded. But I missed the telephone call about that land.

                         ❧

On the same Eggemoggin Reach waters on a far more summer-like afternoon a couple of years later, the day's southwest sailing breeze faded to zephyrs while the sun dropped toward the dark spruces standing tall on Deer Isle. My wife Dianna and I ghosted in our cruising sloop *West Wind* along the north shore of Hog Island. Off a tiny gravel beach below a slope where my father took me as a child to pick cranberries, Dianna steered into what wind remained. I lowered the sails and then the anchor while we savored the silence of the golden late afternoon.

Very close to home, 78-acre Hog Island has always been a favorite destination for daytime picnics and overnight anchoring. The island represents not one but two important stages in the history of island conservation along the Maine coast. During the 1970s the little archipelago at the eastern end of Eggemoggin Reach became a showcase of what could be accomplished by using conservation easements negotiated by Maine Coast Heritage Trust and held, monitored, and enforced by Acadia National Park to preserve the scenic and natural qualities of privately owned islands, preservation in which I am proud to have played a role.

The partnership of Acadia National Park and Maine Coast Heritage Trust, exemplified at Hog Island, truly lit the spark that popularized across the nation conservation easements as a land protection technique. The then owner of Hog, showing great public spirit, gave up his and subsequent owners' rights ever to develop the island. Retaining ownership but giving up development rights, he donated a perpetual, forever wild conservation easement. About thirty years later when Maine Coast Heritage Trust had matured into an organization owning many gems of property as preserves for public enjoyment, a subsequent generous owner gifted the island to the Trust.

With the water surrounding Hog Island glassy and the tide high, Dianna and I slid our stand-up paddleboards over the side and paddled off to circumnavigate the island, enjoying the exercise as well as the sights of the varied shoreline, the woods behind, other islands, and the terns and gulls. In the big cove on the island's far side we discovered kayaks pulled up on the shore. A group of adolescent campers and their counselors, from New Hampshire we learned, had the permission of Maine Coast Heritage Trust to camp overnight. The counselors raved to us about how inspiring it was for all of them to be on such a spectacular island on such a lovely day. Only through these kinds of experiences can a full appreciation of the outdoors and nature be gained. What the New Hampshire group was enjoying on that trip I have been hugely fortunate to have enjoyed throughout my life.

My outdoor adventures on the Maine coast beginning as a child led to deep dedication to Maine—its land-and-seascape and its people. This commitment resulted in 2007 to speaking before the Maine legislature's Joint Standing Committee on Agriculture, Conservation, and Forestry. Governor John Baldacci had nominated me to serve on the

Land for Maine's Future Board. As in many states, Maine voters have several times approved the sale of bonds to fund the purchase of land and conservation easements. The Land for Maine's Future Board is the public body that selects projects to fund. The Joint Standing Committee had to vote whether to recommend to the Maine Senate approval of my nomination, and I was testifying on my own behalf. Part of what I said to the committee that day harked back to the early impact on me of the Maine landscape, before I summarized briefly forty plus years of active land conservation engagement:

> *Land conservation . . . has been my professional and volunteer focus since 1971. I truly attribute the roots of my deep commitment to Maine's extraordinary landscape to childhood summers spent on the shores, waters, and islands of Eggemoggin Reach and then to reinforcement by a marvelous canoe trip down the Allagash River in 1964.*
>
> *Over the years I have been involved in one way or another with just about every type of land of concern to the Land for Maine's Future Board—land for open space conservation; outdoor recreation areas; wildlife and fish habitat; productive farm, blueberry, and forest land; sites for public access to water bodies; and working waterfronts. I have been in the middle of prioritization efforts; landowner and public outreach; negotiations; appraisals; document drafting; raising funds; donations and purchases of fee interests and conservation easements; federal, state, and local tax issues; ensuring local support; and land management. I am familiar with the state and federal agencies as well as the many nonprofits working to conserve Maine land. While my greatest knowledge of Maine land is along the coast, my years on the board of the Forest Society of Maine and a period in the 1990s as the Maine representative of The Conservation Fund deepened my understanding of inland Maine and the North Woods—the land, the people, and the issues.*

The legislature's committee approved my nomination unanimously that day, but three years later I was back for a hearing on my nomination by Governor Baldacci for a second term. I was chuckling by the time I reached home that evening and told Dianna about my day. The Tea Party era had begun, and Land for Maine's Future, with its spending to conserve Maine's natural resources, was not popular with elements of that group. Senator Sherman from Aroostook County, who had voted in my favor at my first hearing, bored in on me in 2010 as I finished testifying on my own behalf. Naïvely as one not experienced in the State House, I had not realized that my mentioning the Brookings Institution in front of Senator Sherman would be like waving a red flag before a bull. Said I, "The 2006 Brookings Institution report stated that Maine '. . . should continue to invest urgently in protecting its top-notch quality of place. . . .'"

As soon as I finished my testimony, Senator Sherman was firing questions. He clearly viewed the Brookings Institution as left-wingers carrying no credence with him. He and an acolyte on the committee from the House voted against me. The remaining Republican voted for me as did all the Democrats, who held the majority. No doubt, the votes against me were more an expression against the program than against me personally, but I came home amused that I could claim to be controversial.

Despite the political pushback received at the hearing, I stand by my support of what the Brookings Institution said. I am in good company. In 2007 the prestigious Governor's Council on Maine's Quality of Place in its first report followed up the Brookings Institution with the statement that quality of place is " . . . Maine's *chief* economic asset." The Council went on, "People with skills . . . can live anywhere. Our research shows they are most interested in living somewhere with a high Quality of Place. This is our most powerful advantage in the global marketplace for people."

That conservation, very much including preserving public access to beautiful places, should be important to all citizens was underscored by a quote in the *Bangor Daily News* from a longtime colleague, Alan Brooks, retiring after a stellar land conservation career in easternmost Maine. According to the newspaper, Alan mentioned that he would never forget a comment made by a woman of limited means: "She was from a low-income background and said to me, 'Until we went to a favorite picnic spot and found a chain across the road, we never felt poor.'"

In the populist atmosphere of the State House I chose not to dwell during my hearings on how my other passion, sailing and the sea, had sparked and enhanced my conservation interests, making my boating and conservation activities inextricably linked. Rowboats and sailboats I began handling at an early age along with learning the whys and wherefores of winds and tides. The boats gave me unbounded aesthetic and sporting pleasure. There was no better place to nourish such interests than among the spruce and fir-covered islands of Eggemoggin Reach with their granite shores and rocky beaches; on the waters that so sparkle in the fresh northwesters after cold fronts; in the gray blankets of mysterious, dripping fog that can obscure everything; or in acquaintance and friendship with hardy, self-reliant people whose roots in this land-and-seascape go back generations. All led to early addiction to this special place on our planet, and I was as drawn to a boating life as the Water Rat in *Wind in the Willows,* who so famously declared that "there is NOTHING—absolutely nothing—half so much worth doing as simply messing about in boats."

2

EARLY EXPOSURE TO BOATS,
PEOPLE, AND ISLANDS

My very existence and presence in Maine might be said to trace to the tragedy of a German machine gun bullet's striking down my grandfather as he led his troops on the killing fields of France only ten days before the Armistice ending the First World War. He had been a rising young Baltimore attorney who had strongly advocated for the United States to enter the war. When it did, he felt duty-bound at age thirty-four to leave behind his wife and three little boys and accept a commission as an infantry officer. Following his death my grandmother, seeking escape from the stifling heat of Baltimore summers, found her way to the Maine coast and settled into an old farmhouse on the shore of Brooklin's Center Harbor. Not long thereafter my mother's parents bought the abutting house, and at age twelve my parents met right there. That hillside overlooking the extraordinarily beautiful islands and waters of Eggemoggin Reach remains the home of my soul.

In my journey from infant to young adult in the two decades immediately following the Second World War, Maine meant summer days in Brooklin. This small and quiet coastal town was then best known to the world, to the extent that it was known at all, as the adopted home of E. B. White, where the old New England barn behind his house provided the setting for his beloved *Charlotte's Web*. My time in Maine was necessarily limited through those years because my father was a businessman in Manhattan, and our primary home and my elementary schooling were there, not in Maine, where I would have vastly preferred to be.

Exposed from my earliest days to both the magnificent coastal scenery and the recreational opportunities afforded by the sheltered waters and good sailing winds of the Reach, the paths that my interests took are hardly surprising. My father had arrived in Brooklin with no nautical experience, but at age eleven or thereabouts he apparently gained access to an old rowboat, a mast, and a sail probably sewed by his mother. He named that first simple craft *Osprey*. To this day ospreys are a constant, fascinating, and often noisy presence in the harbor during the summer months, nesting at the top of a spruce on Chatto Island, the island that provides protection for the harbor. Dad never lost his love for sailing on Eggemoggin Reach, a passion that he had no trouble passing on to me.

My best memories of childhood are of crowding just as much sailing as possible into joyous summer days. I was always the child in the harbor who sailed by far the most, going out virtually every morning and afternoon, wind and weather permitting. My sailing began in Brutal Beasts, a class of small wooden, centerboard catboats (one sail only) that seemed over-the-hill even in my youngest days. They had been brought to Brooklin and nearby Blue Hill at some point before my time after being nearly worn out in their original home waters of Marblehead, Massachusetts.

I was not a self-confident youngster, but in the Brutal Beasts I gained confidence in my nautical skills and developed self-respect—even enough confidence at age thirteen to attract my first girlfriend after meeting her on the rescue boat following my capsize in a race. My family was not a risk-taking family, yet my parents permitted me to sail alone in a Brutal Beast in high wind conditions. They seemed to accept my share of close calls, swampings, the capsize, and a broken mast. I am hugely grateful for those days as a young sailor challenging myself in windy conditions and testing the limits of my own and the boat's capabilities.

The shallow vee shape of a Brutal Beast's bottom meant that with centerboard raised and rudder removed, it was easy to land on a beach. Just a short sail across sheltered waters from Center Harbor are two islands joined at low tide by a long, sweeping sandbar. Often on sunny days a fleet of Brutal Beasts carrying family and friends would rendezvous on this sandbar for memorable picnics. Swimming in the bracingly cold water, exploring the island shores, and searching in the shallows for sand dollars kept us children well entertained while adults prepared the sandwiches. The picnics on those and neighboring islands played a major role in developing my love for Maine islands, an enthusiasm that later led directly to professional land conservation work following my immediate post-college years as a destroyer officer.

The other class of small sailboats to which I was fortunate to have access as a youngster was the well-known Herreshoff 12½. Many traditionalists still consider this 1914 Nathanael Herreshoff design the best small sailboat of all time. They are fun to sail for people who enjoy the heft and predictability of a full-keel, heavy boat as opposed to the quickness of a modern, light, dinghy-type boat. The heavy keel makes them very resistant to swamping and consequently quite safe when properly handled.

The wooden 12½ that Dad chartered each summer was a wonderful training platform. Herreshoff-designed and -built boats are exquisite works of art, both in beauty and craftsmanship, and I was fortunate to become acquainted as a youngster with such nautical gems and at a scale to which I as a child could relate. Among the islands of Eggemoggin Reach in a Herreshoff 12½ I absorbed the joys and rewards of both nature's art form of great landscapes and the nautical art form of lovely sailboats created by human genius.

I was not native to this Maine landscape to which I became and remain so attached. I was a "summer person," a person "from away." When the weather turned cold and the days shortened, we left. Much as I yearned to belong to this Maine scene that I loved, I understood that I could not be what I was not. I was not the "Downeaster" whose family had lived and worked here for centuries. I had not gone to school here with others in town. I did not speak with a Yankee twang—even though at times I tried.

I knew that parochialism in a small New England town could be extreme, a fact vividly illustrated to me by an obituary that I once read in the *Bangor Daily News* under the headline "Franklin Man Dies." Franklin is a small, nearby town, and the deceased was ninety or thereabouts. Reading the obituary I learned that the man had been born in Franklin but moved to the abutting town of Sullivan at age seven and lived in Sullivan ever after. Yet at death he was still a "Franklin man," not a Sullivan man. "As Mainers know, it takes a long time to be a native," said University of Maine professor Dr. Paul Drummond in a lecture about honeybees, a non-native bee introduced from Europe in 1624 and still considered non-native. In Maine, people's origins often are viewed through the same lens.

Also illustrating sometimes slow acceptance of newcomers was my experience with the owner of a small-town general store in the years immediately after moving year-round to Mount Desert Island in the spring of 1972. I often stopped in for milk, bread, and the like, and during the first year the owner, while courteous, gave little indication that he knew who I was. The second year he would smile in recognition but not say much. And then one day the third year he called me Ben and continued into conversation. I liked him from the beginning and accepted that moving into the community was a process best not hurried, but I was relieved finally to have launched an enjoyable relationship, which lasted until he died.

The people that inhabit landscapes are crucial parts of those landscapes. As a child I observed and absorbed the genuine respect and affection which my family felt for residents of Brooklin and the surrounding area. We recognized that many, many local people exhibited highly admirable traits of hard work, great skill in their chosen fields of work, frugality, independence of thought, devotion to family, and general kindness. My grandmother in her last years was dependent on people who cooked her meals, made sure that she had enough firewood, and checked to see if she had other needs. They never failed her. What really gained my notice and respect early was how many people were jacks-of-all trades with a surprisingly broad array of skills, seemingly able to build and repair houses and boats, repair cars and farm equipment, fish, raise food, do woods work, and accomplish whatever else was required to get by in a rural coastal Maine town that was far more rural and economically strapped in my childhood than it is today. City and suburban people whom I knew depended on others for much of what rural Mainers could do for themselves.

I have never developed such a wide array of skills, but I have borne in mind the example set by Maine neighbors, especially as I have pursued my boat interests. I have tried to learn what I needed to know to operate the boats that I have had and to do some of the maintenance on the larger boats and most of the maintenance on the small ones. As an adult, I have chuckled at how my majoring in American colonial history at Harvard little prepared me for being soaked in diesel fuel working on an engine—or a host of other hands-on tasks that I have tackled afloat and ashore.

I was launched into daysailing in small boats as a child, but I also received my introductions to the joys of overnight cruising under sail relatively early. Except for one overnight on a 30-footer when I was six, I began cruising the Maine coast when I was twelve. That summer my Uncle Dick and Aunt Betsy chartered for a week the Maine Coast–class yawl *Snowflake*, a traditional 37-footer designed and built by Farnham Butler of Mount Desert Island. Years later Farnham, a man of delightfully strong opinions, and I would know each other well. He was not only a yacht builder and designer but also a member of the planning board of the town of Mount Desert. We enjoyed long discussions and arguments about both boats and land use.

My kind uncle and aunt chose to use their precious days with *Snowflake* by filling her up with sons and nephews and taking all five of us young ones off to savor the delights of cruising Penobscot Bay. What a great time we had—even seemingly the adults, for we all cruised together on *Snowflake* for a couple of more summers after that. I adored handling the substantial boat, the lovely island anchorages, explorations ashore, and all the mini-adventures and misadventures. Best of all was the camaraderie, undoubtedly the finest aspect of sailing when the crew is congenial.

Aunt Betsy recognized how much I reveled in those days on *Snowflake*. She turned to me in the cockpit one afternoon as we smoked up Penobscot Bay before the wind and seas of a strong southwester, saying, "Benny" (I was called that in those days), "when I am old, I am going to come cruising with you in your yawl." Sadly, cancer cancelled that plan, but the idea and later the memory of it have always meant a great deal.

Snowflake gave so many members of the family so much fun that

Dad decided to buy a cruising boat. Off we went to Essex, Connecticut, one September morning in 1958 to inspect *Arcturus*, one of the Sam Crocker–designed New Bedford 35 sloops. Similar to *Snowflake*, *Arcturus* was a traditional family cruising boat typical of the 1930s and 1940s in New England—wood, heavy displacement, full keel, narrow by modern standards, and comfortable in a seaway. High bulwarks combined with pleasing sheer gave both boats a very seagoing appearance. The fine old gentleman selling *Arcturus*, after lovingly maintaining and cruising her for twenty years, told Dad to count his pennies. Dad did, and he bought her.

The prospect of sailing *Arcturus* to Maine the following spring kept me excited all through the ensuing winter. To sail *all* the way from Connecticut to Maine was a grand adventure. We made a fun trip of it in late June and early July, and my addiction to boats became that much worse.

We sailed and cruised *Arcturus* locally as much as we could. That first summer we had spectacular weather for my first venture to Roque Island, the Cow Yard, and other parts of the delightful cruising waters east of Schoodic Point. When I was fifteen, Dad, away at work, agreed to permit me to skipper *Arcturus* on a short cruise in Penobscot Bay in company with *Snowflake*, again under charter to Uncle Dick. Longtime family friend Artie Howe, then Dean of Admissions at Yale, would stay on *Arcturus* with me. In retrospect, I am not sure whether this requirement was to ensure adult supervision or to increase my chances of being admitted to Yale. I may not have helped my chances for Yale by ordering avid fisherman Artie not to clean his mackerel on *Arcturus*'s teak decks—but I never applied to Yale anyway.

During the 1960s when Dad and I were often on the Reach together on family sails, Dad was also thinking about how to preserve the scenic and natural qualities of the Maine islands. He helped The Nature Conservancy raise money for its first Maine island purchase, Turtle Island off Winter Harbor, in 1963. Incorporated in 1951 as a Washington,

D.C.–based nonprofit organization, The Nature Conservancy was still a small organization in 1963 trying to take advantage of opportunities to preserve important open space cherished by local supporters. It was still years away from being the very large entity, driven by science and policy and globally vital to both land and ocean conservation, that it is today.

Dad and Mother owned Chatto Island at Center Harbor. They and the owners of neighboring islands were in occasional discussion in those years about the possibility of creating a trust to own the islands at the eastern end of Eggemoggin Reach. That was well before the term land trust came into common use. The Eggemoggin Reach island owners were ahead of their time in their conservation thinking. One of these island owners helped fund the purchase of McGlathery Island in Merchant Row off Stonington by Friends of Nature, another early island conservation success.

Both Turtle and McGlathery had been targeted to be pulped for the paper mill then in Bucksport. Harvesting trees on islands, loading the logs onto barges, and towing them to the mill still remained economically viable in that era. An Eggemoggin Reach island, Big Babson, was clear-cut about the same time, and the ugly scar of this denuded Maine island was shocking. Interestingly, it was soon thereafter purchased by conservation-minded owners who granted one of the earliest conservation easements in Maine, which forbid development or any more commercial tree cutting.

That provided the desired scenic and ecological protection, but nearly forty years later in 2010 Dianna and I successfully spearheaded the effort of Maine Coast Heritage Trust to raise funds for a purchase of the 21-acre island at a bargain price from the generous sellers so that it could become a permanent preserve of Maine Coast Heritage Trust. Big Babson is right next to Hog Island, and the two make a magnificent pair of island preserves.

3
DEVELOPING SEA LEGS AND NETWORKS

By the time I was sixteen I longed to expand my sailing and geographic horizons, much as I still loved every minute on home waters. That summer of 1961 I landed my first job, as boatboy and crew. Little did I know at the time that not only was I beginning a series of summer sailing experiences that would teach me a huge amount about sailing and seamanship, but I was about to be introduced into a network of people that would within a few years much enhance my work in Maine coastal conservation.

How I found that first summer job still amazes me by the obsession with boats that it underscored. I was a boarding student at New Hampshire's Phillips Exeter Academy when in the fall of 1960 I used all my free time to mail 800 resumes to sailboat owners on the East Coast, using *Lloyd's Register of American Yachts* as my primary source of names and addresses. I was delightfully astounded—and fellow students opening their mailboxes near mine enviously flabbergasted—at the amount of return mail jamming my mailbox for several days. I surely was in the right place at the right time hunting for a boat job.

All that mail led to several job offers. The job I accepted was with a veteran, skilled cruising sailor named Geoffrey Smith, chairman of a Philadelphia bank. His 38-foot Alden Challenger yawl *Tarna* was one of the early generation of fiberglass auxiliary sailboats. She had a relatively wide, keel-centerboard hull of the type popularized by the famous *Finisterre*, the only boat ever to win three consecutive Newport–Bermuda Races, beginning with the 1956 race. The Cruising Club of America handicap rule then used for racing large sailboats in the United States favored that type of boat, and it would be a type that I would come to know well—racing across the Atlantic in one and, in my thirties, owning one that carried me through the heaviest storms I have encountered in a sailboat at sea. Although long since obsolete in many people's minds, the type remains favored by some sailors as pretty and safe boats with a comfortable motion. They are especially well suited because of shallow draft with centerboard raised to cruising shallow-water areas such as the Bahamas.

The plan for that summer included an entire month roaming the Maine coast. I had never done more than short cruises of a few days, and I was delighted at the prospect of this more extended cruise. We planned to go the full length of the coast to Passamaquoddy Bay at the Canadian border, but that was one of those Maine summers of day after day of fog. Mr. Smith was a fine navigator in the days before sailboats had radar, Loran, or GPS. He navigated with confidence but, nonetheless, wisely gave up the idea of going beyond Schoodic Point. We spent the entire month between Casco Bay and Frenchman Bay, particularly poking up the rivers west of Pemaquid and exploring the islands and coves of Penobscot and Blue Hill Bays. My knowledge of Maine coast geography west of Schoodic vastly expanded. (This was but one of many cruises that helped me so much when exactly ten years later I began work for Maine Coast Heritage Trust in its first year of operation and started actively encouraging owners of islands and key mainland shorefront parcels to consider granting conservation easements in order to preserve in perpetuity their properties' natural and scenic qualities.)

A job I declined for that first summer of marine employment was on the Northeast Harbor–based yawl of Admiral Samuel Eliot Morison, Harvard's legendary maritime historian and the Navy's official historian of World War II. I told a friend, Ned, about the availability of the Morison job, and he took it, perhaps not fully aware of the Admiral's fierce reputation. Ned later told me the story of his scariest moment, only hilarious in hindsight. A high point of the Morison summer each year was entertaining special friends for an island picnic. Mrs. Morison always provided her homemade clam chowder, for which she was renowned. The appointed day arrived with clear skies and brisk northwester, just perfect. Ned was told to be at the house at ten o'clock to pick up the big pot of chowder and take it to the boat, which was on its mooring. As he prepared to place the pot into the dinghy at the float, he tripped, spilling all the chowder into the bilge of the little rowboat. Terrified, he could only think of one remedy—use the boat's bailing sponge to get the chowder back into its pot. The picnic went off without a hitch, the guests reportedly exclaiming about the best-ever chowder.

The siren song of the open ocean called me to venture beyond coastal waters, and crewing on a boat returning after a Bermuda Race was one of the best ways to begin getting offshore experience. Owners often have to scramble for crew for the return trip, the racing crew flying home to return to jobs and families. The summer after being on *Tarna* I was thrilled to be invited to join *Gesture* in Bermuda after that year's race. A 57-foot sloop designed by Olin Stephens and built just after World War II, *Gesture* must rank among the prettiest sailboats of the era. She had proven fast and won her share of races.

I learned a great deal on that passage from Bermuda to Manchester, Massachusetts, but perhaps what struck me most was the wonderful camaraderie that can develop offshore on a sailboat among a congenial crew, reinforcing what I had discovered earlier in summer cruises along the Maine coast. Far from the distractions of land and long before email and satellite phones enabled maintaining distracting ties to land even when at sea, conversations developed a depth I had not experienced before. For those few days at sea the crew developed a genuine closeness built upon mutual respect and affection for each other as human beings. That is one of the great rewards of offshore sailing, as I would rediscover many times.

The weather cooperated in giving me experiences to remember and to learn from. *Gesture* was the largest boat on which I had yet sailed, but I discovered that she looked very small from the bow while changing to a smaller jib as the foredeck was swept by angry seas in a northeast gale. The morning the gale began, a school friend and I sat on deck watching Mother Carey's chickens swooping down the backs of the gray waves. These little seabirds playing in the wild weather inspired us with youthful glee; we anticipated the adventure of the day to come with great excitement. By the time the weather moderated the next day I had learned a lot about what to expect at sea when conditions deteriorate. I would see far worse from the bridge of a destroyer in far parts of the world in a few short years, but my initiation into the ways of the ocean had begun.

That same summer I began crewing on racing yachts by accepting an invitation to sail on Arthur Santry's magnificent Aage Nielsen–designed 57-foot keel-centerboard yawl *Temptation*. Like *Gesture*, *Temptation* was a yacht of lovely lines, gleaming varnish, scrubbed teak decks, and powerful and speedy sailing ability. To me beautiful sailboat hulls are the most exquisite form of sculpture. Several of the Nielsen designs represent my perception of aesthetic perfection—especially *Temptation,* one of my favorite yachts of all time. Under Arthur's demanding guidance while crewing for him for several years, I was to learn a great deal about seamanship, racing tactics, and boat speed, and I was to be shipmates with some outstanding sailors, several of whom had been in the famous 12-meter *Vim* crew of 1958. In that first America's Cup defense since 1937, the aging, pre–World War II *Vim* nearly beat the brand-new, faster *Columbia* for the right to defend the Cup.

The New York Yacht Club Cruise of 1962 was my first taste of just how elegant yachting still was in that era. Early every morning I helped *Temptation*'s fine professional captain, Bun Russell, run a chamois over the on-deck varnish to wipe off the dew before the lens effect of the water droplets could increase the damage of the sun's rays. Of course, as soon as each day's racing concluded, we wiped down the varnish again with fresh water to remove the day's accumulation of salt as quickly as possible. *Temptation*'s immaculate varnish was matched by that of the large wooden Trumpy motoryacht of Arthur's uncle, which served as our tender and alongside of which we lay at night. These were just two of a whole fleet of such extraordinary yachts that in the evenings disgorged scores of blue-blazered men and stylishly dressed women into launches, which ferried them ashore to parties in such ports as Newport, Nantucket, Edgartown, and Marion.

One afternoon after a race the professional captain of a yacht anchored nearby called over, inviting Bun Russell for dinner, and asked, "Would your other hand want to come too?" As Bun's teenaged helper I was the "other hand." Bun's reply stuck in my mind over time as my life became centered in downeast Maine, far removed from the urban scene of New York and Boston and upscale watering holes in between. "No,"

I heard Bun say, "he's one of the high-pressure guys." And, of course, later that afternoon off I went in my own blue blazer to a party ashore.

⚓

Again the next summer I looked beyond my home Maine waters for opportunities afloat and found myself aboard a legendary yacht, the experiences on which I treasure with especially fond memories. The schooner *Nina* was designed by Starling Burgess specifically for the 1928 race from New York to Santander, Spain. He was the same naval architect who had designed the Brutal Beasts I sailed in Brooklin as a youngster. The race to Spain was the first transatlantic race for yachts with amateur crews, and she won that event. By the 1960s *Nina* was the only schooner still racing regularly in the major East Coast races.

She also was one of the larger yachts then racing. She was 59 feet on deck, but because of her long bowsprit the length of her rig was 70 feet. In 1928 she had been considered a relatively small yacht, but by the sixties the Depression, followed by World War II and the income tax, had eliminated many of the larger yachts, although new and much larger yachts appeared later in the twentieth century as new fortunes were made. Highly innovative when first launched, *Nina* was one of the first schooners to race with a staysail schooner rig, in which the gaff sail on the foremast is replaced by a triangular staysail on a boom akin to a jib and above it a quadrilateral sail that hoists to both mastheads.

I first stepped aboard *Nina* in Annapolis the afternoon before the start of the 1963 Annapolis to Newport Race. To say that I was nervous is an understatement. This was to be my first ocean race, and I was crewing on one of the most famous yachts then racing. I was determined to prove to all aboard and to myself that I could acquit myself well.

The test of the next few days turned out to be not of my sailing skill but of my ability to achieve a workable relationship with *Nina's* highly respected, tough Norwegian professional captain, Teddy Thorson. Teddy maintained *Nina* magnificently, and he was fiercely loyal to his boss, owner DeCoursey Fales, known to one and all as Commodore since his term in that role at the New York Yacht Club. For me, though, in those first few days Teddy was the drill sergeant and I was the raw recruit. Doing his bidding was almost impossible until I had spent enough time with him to begin to understand his heavily Norwegian-accented English. The more excited he became, the more Norwegian his words sounded.

Until an opportunity arose in Newport to earn his respect and gratitude, I found that I could never satisfy Teddy—or Captain Thorson as I called him during the first difficult days. He reached his rudest one afternoon en route to Newport while we were running under spinnaker in light, fluky air. I was at the foremast frequently adjusting the spinnaker pole height to keep the spinnaker's shape as efficient as possible. The growling bear, as I then thought of Teddy, was off watch in his bunk under my feet. After enduring the noise of the pole adjustments for some time, Teddy suddenly threw up the forward hatch, barking, "Vould you get de f___ aft! You sail dis *Nina* like a goddam dinghy!" I retreated to the chuckling of the rest of the watch, who all had had to go through their own break-in times with Teddy.

I endured Teddy to Newport, wondering how much more racing I really wanted to do on *Nina*. I so much enjoyed my times with Bun Russell, *Temptation*'s captain, that Teddy's hostility took me totally by surprise. Furthermore, I have rarely had trouble getting along with shipmates and new acquaintances. Following our tying up in Newport all except me either headed for home or went ashore for an evening of post-race revelry. Exhausted I climbed into my bunk for some good sleeping while the boat was deserted. In the middle of the night I was awakened by a loud thud on deck followed by groans. Eventually, Teddy dragged himself to his bunk in the forecastle. Teddy's head was killing him when we arose in the morning, yet he had to face the post-race task of scrubbing *Nina*'s vast expanse of teak decks. I took pity on the subdued Teddy that morning and offered to stay aboard for the day and do the job. Teddy gratefully collapsed back into his bunk while I went to work on my hands and knees with the bronze wool. In late afternoon Teddy signaled his appreciation and his accepting me into *Nina*'s crew by inviting me forward to join the yacht's steward and himself for cherry pie, Teddy's favorite. After that I really enjoyed sailing with Teddy and took his growling in stride.

Owner DeCoursey Fales was as warm and easy to get along with as Teddy was difficult. He always had a twinkle in his eye, loved to make his crew laugh, and took great delight in being slightly naughty, doing things that he knew would not fully meet the approval of his beloved wife, a most gracious and lovely woman. The rest of us were all on our best behavior when Mrs. Fales was aboard. Late every afternoon she liked to have the professional steward unroll a small Persian rug on the main cabin sole and serve tea with English biscuits and jam. That was a pleasant affair for all aboard that certainly set a vastly different tone from what I had been used to on sailboats.

Far stronger than *Nina*'s tea were the martinis served immediately upon finishing a race regardless of the hour, day or night. We finished one race at Stamford, Connecticut, just after daybreak. The martinis we dumped on our cornflakes. My drive up the Connecticut Thruway an hour or two later was not something to repeat.

Our most successful race of the 1963 season was the Marblehead to Halifax Race. *Nina* loved to reach with the wind angle on the beam because her schooner rig enabled her to set an enormous cloud of sail in those conditions. We had fast reaching all the way to Halifax. Off-watch I lay in my bunk in thick fog listening to the water flying by the wooden planking next to my ear at 10 to 12 knots. We saw nothing all through the race until after the finish, heading up Halifax Harbour, we suddenly emerged from that dungeon-like Scotia fog into bright morning sunshine. A launch full of newspaper reporters and television cameras came alongside with the thrilling news that not only were we first to finish, but we had broken the course record by five hours.

Nina's long racing career ended in 1966 with her entering Hamilton Harbour, Bermuda, flags at half-staff following being hailed by the Newport to Bermuda Race committee boat at the finish line with the sad news that DeCoursey Fales, stricken just before the start and not aboard, had died in a New York hospital. I had raced to Bermuda that year on another boat, and those of us there knew that we would never again see *Nina* charging through a racing fleet. Under other owners a cruising life continued for the grand old lady of the sea until 2013, when *Nina* made international headlines by tragically vanishing with all hands while crossing the Tasman Sea separating New Zealand and Australia.

❧

School and college summers cruising and racing with people like the Commodore greatly expanded my network of contacts up and down the East Coast. My interest in sailing and boats gave us common ground, and not a small number of the people whom I came to know loved Maine, whether they owned property on the Maine coast or simply visited on their boats. Not only did my sailing help me in my later conservation work by expanding my knowledge of the geography of the Maine coast, but the contacts that I developed through sailing proved very helpful. Many of the people leading Maine coast conservation efforts liked nothing better than cruising among the islands and bays. Partly because of my sailing I came to their attention.

With sailing as a shared interest and my knowledge of the coast's geography giving me credibility, I was offered the opportunity to engage professionally in land conservation a few years after those summers of cruising and racing. Once into that field my sailing contacts proved helpful in reaching out to owners of important Maine properties and in cultivating people who might financially support conservation efforts.

My focus until the mid-1960s remained on the sailing, however, not on the conservation work that would follow later. One of my never-dying dreams as a teenager was to participate in a transatlantic race. My chance arrived in January of my senior year at Harvard when Danny Burnes, one of several brothers with whom I was friends at college, appeared in my dorm room. Would I like to crew on his father's *Adele* in the coming summer's race from Bermuda to Copenhagen? Would I! By that year of 1966 the Vietnam War was heating up. I was already enrolled to enter Navy Officer Candidate School at Newport in September, and in my last free summer I hoped to do as much sailing as possible. As it turned out, I was able to race in both the Block Island and Bermuda Races on one boat, *Vivace*, and then switch in Bermuda to *Adele*, which was a sistership. Both were Ted Hood–designed 45-foot keel-centerboarders, larger but similar in design to *Tarna*, on which I had my first job.

The week in Bermuda between races proved enjoyable but also gave time for introspection. More than once I rode my rented motorbike to St. David's Head and, gazing out over the ocean, thought about how in just a few days I would be setting off across that ocean for the 3,600 miles to Copenhagen. Sometimes I felt a tightening in my stomach. I had never sailed on *Adele* or with the Burneses. My longest offshore passage was the Newport to Bermuda Race. Was I mentally prepared to face the whole North Atlantic? During that week I was not sure.

In the final days before the start I spent much of the time helping with final preparations on *Adele*, almost the last task being loading tins of bread. Pepperidge Farm had taken orders from the fleet long before. The afternoon before the start Rad Daley, a former shipmate from *Nina* who worked for Pepperidge Farm, flew to Bermuda with the bread and in a chartered launch delivered the tins to the assembled boats. Rad's hearty farewell and that delicious bread's being tucked into lockers were reassuring, and by the time all was stowed on that last evening, I was eager to be on our way the next afternoon.

Even in summer Bermuda weather can be atrocious. On the day of the start a northeast gale with driving rain lashed the island. The long trip under power from Hamilton Harbour around to the start in the ocean off St. David's Head was wet and cold. Once out of the protection of the reefs the seas were large, and the wind was over 30 knots. By the time we crossed the starting line in late afternoon hard on the wind in that gale, we and most everything below were soaked. During my first off-watch that evening, hanging on in my soggy bunk as it rose and fell and the bow smashed into the waves, I tried to keep my face out from under the dripping porthole overhead. I had never been seasick, but that evening I knew what queasiness meant and the cold and depression that can accompany it. Others on board were feeling far worse. We pounded on through the wet, windy night.

Moderating winds and delightful sunshine the next day cheered us all up and dried out the boat. I began to settle into enjoying an experience of a lifetime. For this race, owner and skipper Bunny Burnes had included among his eight-man crew four of his sons, ranging in age from mid-teens to mid-twenties, and me. We probably had the youngest crew in the race, and I found the whole Burnes tribe most congenial and great fun.

The transatlantic race was a very different experience from a shorter race like the Bermuda Race–the difference between a sprint and a marathon. The day after day of going on watch, then back to the bunk, on watch, then back to the bunk made one feel suspended in time, not unlike the less pleasant experience I would have the next year on a Navy destroyer, of watch after watch, day after day of round-the-clock gunfire support missions along the coast of Vietnam. The wear and tear on *Adele* in the transatlantic was much more extensive than on a shorter race. We used to make up songs about driving the boat until she broke, then fixing her and driving her until she broke again. Chafed sheets and halyards, blown-out spinnakers, and broken steering gear were very much part of the race on *Adele*. The wear and tear on the gear added greatly to crew fatigue, for often the off-watch had to make repairs instead of sleep while the watch on deck sailed.

Crossing the North Atlantic in a sailboat was a marvelous lesson in ocean currents, weather systems, and geography. The first faceful of frigid Labrador Current water when coming on watch late one evening after the days of warm seas north of Bermuda showed how sharp can be the dividing line between an ocean current and the contiguous water. Four straight days of spinnaker running in zero visibility fog off Newfoundland brought home how densely the cold northern waters condense the moisture in the warm air masses that flow up from the south.

We were required to leave Point Alpha, a position in the ocean supposedly safely outside any iceberg danger, to port. Point Alpha was a reminder of all those bergs that calve off the glaciers of Labrador and Greenland and drift south until totally melted away. Our course to Scandinavia took us between the Orkney and Shetland Islands north of Scotland. On a gray afternoon we slipped by Fair Isle in the middle of that passage, its great cliffs rising to rolling moors. This was the first land that we had seen since Bermuda over two weeks earlier. Then a painfully cold sail across the North Sea brought us to Scandinavian waters and on to the finish line off the northern tip of Denmark twenty-two days after the start in Bermuda.

The race from Bermuda to Copenhagen capped the years of crewing for a series of fine skippers on wonderful boats with skilled and congenial shipmates. Those summers during school and college were treasures. I have been fortunate to sail many miles since then, mostly on my own boats. My apprenticeships on the yachts of others gave me invaluable experience, taught me many lessons, and introduced me to a host of accomplished people, including some I would see again in later conservation work.

⚓

After the transatlantic and a few following weeks back home in Brooklin, I had to take a long break both from Maine and from sailing. Maine's initiating me to the saltwater world had led me to choose the Navy as the way to meet post-college national service requirements during the Vietnam War. The final decision to apply to Navy Officer Candidate School early in my senior year in college exemplifies how the wisdom of elders can fortuitously guide young people in life-changing ways.

Every so-called "House," really dormitory, at Harvard was under the supervision of a distinguished professor known as the "Master." At the beginning of the academic year, Master Finlay of Eliot House summoned each senior to discuss post-college plans. When my turn came, I went to his lovely Eliot House apartment, furnished as one might expect with appropriate antiques and silver. Master Finlay was an elderly classics professor, the son of an earlier Harvard professor, with chiseled handsomeness, thick white hair, and an upper-crust accent fit for a movie. "So, Ben, what are your plans for next year?" he crisply queried over a cup of afternoon tea.

"I'm thinking of applying for a secondary school teaching and coaching position," I replied, considering history and rowing as two areas of perhaps adequate expertise. Master Finlay, someone with such a lifelong commitment to teaching, scowled noticeably and asked, "Do you have any other ideas?"

"Yes," said I. "I've had friends who went to Navy Officer Candidate School, then were assigned to destroyer duty. They liked it, and I'm thinking of applying to Officer Candidate School."

The scowl vanished. Master Finlay, pointing his finger at me, exclaimed, "That is what you should do!" The very next morning I arranged for my Navy physical. Master Finlay had invaluably steered me toward what I most needed, exposure to a much broader world of people and experiences.

Thousands upon thousands of miles of destroyer steaming followed, first as the combat information center officer, then as the navigator, and taught me a whole new set of lessons about the sea, world politics, and people. I much enjoyed being on the ocean in all its moods, whether watching the dark green peaks of Oahu rise above the horizon in a perfect dawn, thousands of dolphins leap high into the air above a calm Persian Gulf, or huge waves off Madagascar crash against the bridge windows 40 feet above the ocean's surface. From that destroyer, *USS New* (DD 818), I saw many coastlines and realized all the more how special is our Maine coast.

4

AFLOAT IN THE GLARE
OF THE FIRST EARTH DAY

I completed Navy active duty and returned to civilian life in the fall of 1969 with a lifelong recognition of the importance and benefits of national service, my appreciation for which has grown even stronger in recent years. A prescription to begin healing the deep divisions in our highly polarized nation today might include enlisting more young adults in national service opportunities—whether in the military or in civilian programs. Working with and depending upon people from all parts of the country and from all walks of life should go a long way toward increasing empathy for others as well as instilling pride in our shared national heritage.

Release from active duty came too late to start graduate study the same year. Young and unencumbered, I and my wife of a few months, Judy Wallace, whom I began dating in Boston when we were both college seniors, eagerly looked forward to a year of freedom. I wanted the year to be constructive and began searching for a job in conservation. My appreciation of the natural world that had developed in Maine had expanded as I traveled and saw other beautiful places and saw too the damage that man has done. I grew to realize that no place is safe—that overpopulation, human nature, and economic need and greed could scar any area. Realizing the imperative of mounting vigorous opposition to accelerating environmental degradation and applauding the efforts of people who did, I wanted to join them.

Fortunate circumstances were about to permit combining my conservation and sailing interests—and, fortuitously, in the year of the massive publicity garnered by the first Earth Day. When I went to Boston to call on Dr. Charles H. W. (Hank) Foster, founder of the New England Natural Resources Center, he posed me a challenge that I could hardly refuse. A great believer that people of every sort of interest

and talent can contribute to environmental protection, he quickly ferreted out my enthusiasm for sailing. What would I think, he asked, of
undertaking a project to encourage greater participation by New England yacht clubs in coastal conservation? He had long thought that
not only the size of the boating fraternity but the talent, experience,
influence, funds, and interest in the sea of so many of the members
seemed to give yacht clubs tremendous potential to assist in coastal
protection. If I drew up a satisfactory project prospectus, Hank Foster
would attempt to arrange sponsorship.

The result of his challenge led to a great outlet for the environmental idealism of Judy and me. Probably more importantly, we were
about to receive excellent experience in the promotion and marketing
of conservation ideas, training that by the following year I would apply
directly to professional conservation work along the Maine coast.

After preparing the prospectus and while awaiting a definite answer,
Judy and I began to think more and more about trying to fit a significant cruise into the coming months. Then the light bulb went on. Why
not, we wondered, combine the two ideas of a cruise and promoting
yacht club conservation efforts? We could carry our message the length
of the East Coast, and traveling by boat rather than car would stimulate
vastly more yacht club interest. The pieces of the project came together
quickly. The American Littoral Society of Sandy Hook, New Jersey,
agreed that we could sail under its flag. In its own words the American
Littoral Society "seeks to empower people to care for the coast through
advocacy, conservation, and education."

Under the Society's auspices we would meet with officers of major
yacht clubs to discuss ways that clubs could become active in coastal
conservation. Some of our recommendations would be to engage in
the preservation of natural areas, to publicize threats to local waters
and shores to all members and the community at large, to actively
participate in political issues affecting the coastal environment, and to
include training about the ecology of the local area in junior activities.
We would also survey coastal environmental problems and maintain a
photographic record for lecture purposes. Judy's background as a jour-
nalism major in college, with work experience in both publications and

elementary school teaching, and as a talented amateur photographer would stand us in good stead.

In Fort Lauderdale, Florida, we located a boat that sounded perfect for our cruise, a 31-foot wooden yawl of the International 500 class, designed by the well-regarded Robert Henry, Jr., and built in Germany. The International 500s were exceptionally pretty, fast, and responsive under sail. In fact, they are one of the very nicest boats of that size that I have ever seen. Despite lovely varnished mahogany topsides, this particular boat was in considerably less pristine condition than the magazine advertisement for her had led us to believe. She suffered from several years of careless maintenance. The professional surveyor found no serious defects, however, and she could go cruising right away, leaving until later correcting cosmetic and dry rot issues. The boat was full of cockroaches and her bunk cushions were covered with German Shepherd hairs, but we were young and adaptable. We even put up with the roaches until months later when we arrived home in Maine.

We named our little yawl *Eggemoggin* after our home waters of Eggemoggin Reach. In the Abenaki language *eggemoggin* means "fish-weir place." Indeed the Native Americans apparently used to set fish traps, or weirs, in the shallows between Deer Isle and Little Deer Isle on the south side of Eggemoggin Reach. The name seemed appropriate for a vessel whose mission would be to promote protection of the natural coastal environment.

❧

We moved aboard with not only clothes, food, and tools but cameras, typewriter, tape recorder, and boxes of books also. We were quickly ready to go but delayed commencing the American Littoral Society project long enough for a ten-day dash across the Gulf Stream and back for what turned out to be a very windy early March exploration of the Abaco Islands in the northern Bahamas. I have been fortunate to cruise the charming Abacos a number of times since in other boats, but I have never again been pinned on a shallow lee shore as we were at Powell Cay for forty-eight hours following passage of a cold front, praying that the two anchors would hold in winds that at times were hitting 40 to 50 knots. We tried to ease the strain on the anchors with the engine in the worst of it and prayed that there would always be enough water under our keel at low tide as the boat pitched violently. What an introduction to Bahamas cruising—and the lesson about being very cautious of strong winter cold fronts in the Bahamas was never to be forgotten.

Except for our cruise to the Bahamas, we stayed in the Intracoastal Waterway all the way from Florida to Norfolk, Virginia. The need to observe coastal conditions as closely as possible and the many stops we must make in connection with our project precluded sailing north in the ocean. Maintained by the Army Corps of Engineers, the Intracoastal Waterway provides a protected passage from Miami to Norfolk, utilizing rivers, creeks, canals, and sounds. In Florida the Waterway channel is often within a mile of the Atlantic beaches, separated from the ocean by the long, narrow, sandy islands that stretch along most of that state's east coast. Occasional inlets give access to the open sea.

Heading north in the Intracoastal Waterway from Fort Lauderdale, we saw why this section was called the "Gold Coast." Hundred-foot yachts lay alongside the docks of Fort Lauderdale's largest and plushest marina, Bahia Mar. Uniformed crews waved as we passed by. Modern, glass-fronted homes nestling among palm trees overlooked the Waterway and innumerable side canals. Each house had a carefully manicured lawn, and most had docks with boats tied to them. Farther along we passed the high-rise buildings of Pompano Beach and later an enormous hotel at Boca Raton that resembled nothing so much as a pink castle.

To create the waterfront real estate on which to build their houses, hotels, and marinas, Florida developers filled millions of acres of mangrove swamps. Dredging canals through the swamps, the developers dumped the dredging to either side, then brought in more fill by barge and truck. When finally the surface of the filled area was sufficiently above high tide, seawalls or bulkheads were built to prevent the fill from washing back into the canals. Not until north of Palm Beach did we see land in its original state; between Fort Lauderdale and Palm Beach we found virtually every acre developed.

When we stopped at Jupiter Island, a day's run north of Palm Beach, to talk to Nat Reed, then aide for conservation to the Governor of Florida and later Assistant Secretary of the Interior for Parks and Wildlife, he spoke a great deal about the mangrove swamps destroyed by the developers and about the ecological importance of estuarine areas in general. Nat Reed and his family spearheaded efforts to preserve natural habitat at Jupiter Island and across Hobe Sound from the island. Four miles of the western shore of Hobe Sound had been given to the U.S. Fish and Wildlife Service, and the Reed family had donated to the National Audubon Society a major portion of the undeveloped northern end of Jupiter Island.

Leaving Nat Reed and Jupiter Island astern, little did I suspect that he and I would cross tracks again years later in the context of my involvement in trying to conserve land near the Schoodic District of Maine's Acadia National Park. He and his family spend summers in Winter Harbor close by Acadia, and he has been an important supporter of restoring the salmon run in the Penobscot River through dam removal. There would be a lot of water under the keel—or over the dam—before we encountered each other in Maine.

Our usual approach to yacht club commodores was to mail ahead a letter of explanation about our mission along with a questionnaire. When we followed up by telephone to try to arrange to get together, we found that the receptions we received ran the gamut. In Daytona the commodore reacted with unmasked suspicion and refused to meet at the club, for he could not "expose the club." In Jacksonville the commodore was most cordial on the first telephone call but became unavailable after a newspaper reporter called him about us before we could telephone back to make final arrangements for a meeting. In the Chesapeake we began to receive much more cordial welcomes from commodores and other interested yacht club members. They briefed us extensively on their views of the Chesapeake problems and took us to lunch, invited us to their homes for dinner, and, in Annapolis, took us racing in the Wednesday evening series.

Perhaps the bluntest commodore was Richard Nye, commodore of one of the major Long Island Sound yacht clubs. He had established a legendary reputation for his ocean racing successes on both sides of the Atlantic with several yachts named *Carina*, for which reason I held him in considerable awe. Crusty and well along in years, he showed little interest in our mission and none in getting his club involved in promoting better care of local shores and waters. He told me how Long Island Sound had become so dirty that it was disgusting, to use his word, then went on to say, "I'm glad someone is calling 'Halt!'—but don't expect me to carry the cudgel."

We stopped at nearly fifty yacht clubs along the East Coast. In order to translate our proposals into specific recommendations, we needed a thorough knowledge of the issues confronting each area through which we passed. To that end we spoke with scores of people representing a wide array of interests and expertise—not only recreational boaters but also conservationists, fishermen (both commercial and sport), businessmen, educators, and others.

We were always interested in the first environmental problem mentioned by the people to whom we talked. In Florida, more often than not, dredging and filling of swamps and marshes first came to people's minds. In the Chesapeake water pollution and siltation was a major concern, not only the industrial and urban pollution near the major cities but also the negative impacts from farming. Farmers were plowing their fields too close to the Chesapeake's myriad creeks and rivers, with the result that rains were washing silt, fertilizers, and pesticides into the creeks. In Maine we heard much about the subdivision and posting of the shorefront, river pollution that in the decades since our trip has been considerably cleaned up, and the threat (so prominent at that time) of major oil port development. People worried that spills along Maine's coast could dwarf the Torrey Canyon and Santa Barbara disasters, which remained so much in the public consciousness in 1970.

We often found that young people were much more attuned to environmental problems than their elders. When we passed through West Palm Beach, we spent a night at Spencer's Yacht Yard, where we tied up next to a powerboat we had seen in the Bahamas. The young couple who served as crew for the Texan owner invited us aboard for a drink. Over rum we explained the mission upon which we were embarked. Roughly our age—mid-twenties—the young couple listened attentively and eagerly asked questions. In contrast, the older owner showed absolutely no interest.

Our proposal for club action that gained the most widespread and enthusiastic encouragement was aimed at children—that clubs should incorporate into their junior programs basic training in the ecology of their local area. In Beaufort, North Carolina, we visited Will Hon, who had demonstrated the feasibility of getting youngsters interested in coastal ecology. He made one point very clear to us: To awaken a child's interest in and appreciation for the natural world, one must instruct the child in terms of his or her own locale, where the child can go out and observe nature.

Will directed a federally funded project to develop marine science materials for the Carteret County public school system. He had written texts for grades one through twelve which, when combined with field trips, stimulated students from all over North Carolina. We accompanied a tenth-grade field trip to a salt marsh and were intrigued as much by the students' obvious fascination as by the life from the marsh that they netted by wading in water up to their necks.

The great salt marshes of the Carolinas and Georgia are extraordinary and have remained a favorite part of the East Coast during subsequent trips over the years on the Intracoastal Waterway. On the Waterway trip in *Eggemoggin* we had a particularly personal encounter with these marshes. We had anchored with bow and stern anchors in a very narrow Georgia creek. The tidal range is almost as much as in Maine— a good 9 feet in Georgia. In the dark of the wee hours of the morning we awoke to find *Eggemoggin* aground in the mud of the creek bottom and beginning to list to one side as the tide receded. Our anchors had been unable to keep us from drifting out of the center of the channel, where the water was deep enough for our nearly 5 feet of draft. By dawn *Eggemoggin* was lying on her bilge with minimal water around the hull. In the glorious sunrise over the marshes we clambered down into the mud for the fun of taking a photo of the boat on her side surrounded by mud and salt marsh grasses.

We lingered for a lovely three weeks in May in the East Coast's largest estuary, the Chesapeake. The banks of the creeks and rivers were in full bloom with lilacs, dogwoods, and azaleas. The wafting scent of lilacs often greeted us as we entered anchorages in the evenings.

From the Chesapeake we pushed on rapidly. One afternoon as we sailed up the Jersey shore, the rail frequently buried by a fresh north-wester, I noticed blue tail feathers at the end of the mizzen boom peeking out from behind the sail. Enticed to the deck by a cup of water which we put on the afterdeck, the blue jay huddled first in the lee of the bulwarks, then under a winch base as the wind piped up. It did not fly off until we finally entered Manasquan Inlet seven hours after coming aboard.

A strong southeast wind on a sunny Memorial Day pushed us by the Statue of Liberty and up the East River past lower Manhattan. We roared through Hell Gate at maximum flood. Our logbook records the parenthetical comment, "Damn rough!"

The green slime, brown scum, and assorted debris of Long Island Sound was the most visible water pollution of our entire journey. Following a look at the aftermath of an oil spill in Bridgeport, we pushed on to the eastward. We stopped at a number of the well-known sailing centers south of Cape Cod. I had not cruised the waters between Fishers Island and Cape Cod since before my Navy days and was very surprised at the increase in the number of pleasure boats in that area between 1965 and 1970. The huge number of masts visible in the harbor as we approached Cuttyhunk Island showed me that the sailing world I had known growing up had changed forever. The advent of fiberglass boats had made boating a mass recreation.

North of the Cape we stopped at Marblehead and Manchester, Massachusetts, before finally setting a course for Maine. Returning to Maine has always thrilled me, even now after almost fifty years of its being my permanent home. Perhaps most indicative of our feelings as we let go the anchor in Kittery is our logbook entry: "MAINE!"

What took us by surprise as we worked our way north was the extensive press interest in our cruise. The publicity about coastal environmental problems that we generated was among the trip's most useful accomplishments. The American Littoral Society had issued a press release about our trip, but I, at least, did not anticipate the extent of interest. We learned, however, that in that original Earth Day spring of 1970 the words "environment" and "conservation" brought reporters running. In Jacksonville, Florida, conservationist friends arranged for our first television coverage. All the while worrying that he and his expensive camera would topple backward into the water off the rickety marina float, a cameraman filmed an interview about the project. Judy and I sat on *Eggemoggin*'s foredeck answering questions, constantly swatting our faces because of swarms of gnats. We never did see how all the fighting off gnats looked on TV, for just as the six o'clock local news went on the air, the marina television set lost its picture.

American Home magazine flew a whole team to Annapolis to spend a day interviewing and filming us for a feature in the magazine. It was all a bit contrived, our having to look scrubbed and clean-cut and Judy's pretending to lower the anchor over the rail while dressed in spotless shore clothes. We got a laugh and a lot of coverage out of the day, though.

When we reached Boston, we did a full-scale press conference at the New England Aquarium and a radio interview. A month or two later we were called back to Boston to describe the voyage and show our slides on a television program.

The publicity generated demand for lectures. Every summer Edgartown on Martha's Vineyard hosts a summer lecture series. We were invited to bring *Eggemoggin* to Edgartown, where we planned to stop anyway, and present one of the summer's lectures. By late July much of our cruise was behind us, and having an extensive collection of slides, we accepted. I have done a great deal of public speaking and lecturing in years since, but I was new to it then. Looking over the roster of summer speakers when we arrived in Edgartown, we gasped, and our stomachs churned. Every other speaker that summer was a major figure in his or her field and well-known. We were green amateurs. We spent the entire afternoon before the evening lecture rehearsing the program over and over. To our amazement our lecture came off to great accolades, and we were high as kites as we sailed over to Woods Hole the next day. We gave the lecture quite a few more times in the following months, one of the most receptive audiences being the entire student body at Massachusetts's Deerfield Academy.

The greatest benefit that we gained from our crusade for coastal conservation was our own broad education in the environmental problems facing the East Coast. The publicity, including magazine articles that I wrote and Judy's excellent photography, reached a great number of people, and that was of benefit. Yacht clubs clearly were not ready to "carry the cudgel" on environmental problems to any great extent, although we did find some that had become involved in such matters as protection of local islands, helping identify point sources of pollution in their harbors, and occasionally writing letters to politicians on a major development proposal that seemed to pose a threat to their home waters. Some individual members of clubs, although acting in other capacities, were actively involving themselves in efforts to protect the waters and shores so critical to their favorite recreation.

In mid-August, ecstatic to be home, we picked up *Eggemoggin*'s mooring in Brooklin, Maine, five months and four days after leaving Fort Lauderdale. Little did I know that a major Maine conservation opportunity was about to be offered to me.

5

THE LAUNCHING OF
MAINE COAST HERITAGE TRUST

Ten days after *Eggemoggin* arrived in Brooklin that August of 1970, I went to an event that changed the course of my life. This was the announcement in the living room of Peggy and David Rockefeller's house in Seal Harbor on Mount Desert Island of the formation of Maine Coast Heritage Trust.

The previous winter, while preparing *Eggemoggin* at a Florida marina for our East Coast conservation cruise under the flag of the American Littoral Society, I had received a call from an elder statesman of the Maine environment. Bob Patterson was a respected Mount Desert Island architect and president of the board of directors of the Natural Resources Council of Maine. He had heard of me and asked whether I would be interested in being considered for the job of executive director of a new organization named Maine Coast Heritage Trust, which was being formed to promote the protection of the scenic and natural qualities of Maine islands. He was helping the founders of this new effort, Peggy Rockefeller and Tom Cabot, with some of the start-up tasks—including, most importantly, working successfully with the Maine legislature to pass a statute authorizing government agencies to accept conservation restrictions. This statute enabled private property owners voluntarily to place permanent development limits on their land. In common usage these restrictions are called "conservation easements."

I certainly was flattered to be asked about my interest in being considered for the job, but we were about to set forth on our sail north and could not focus on anything else just then. More importantly, I had decided that although I doubted that I was headed for a business career, I wanted the training in finance, marketing, administration, and computer use that a Masters of Business Administration degree would provide. I was following up my three years of active duty as a naval officer by commencing the following September the two-year M.B.A. program at Dartmouth's Amos Tuck School of Business Administration.

A meeting for island owners announcing the new Maine Coast Heritage Trust effort was set for August at Peggy and David Rockefeller's home. Mother and Dad were invited, being the owners of Chatto Island in Brooklin. Dad, known to be interested in island conservation as well as acquainted with other island owners in the Eggemoggin Reach area, had spent a winter evening on his hands and knees with Peggy examining nautical charts of the coast and discussing who were the owners of various islands. That evening is presumably when Peggy heard about my recent return to civilian life and my conservation interests. She asked Bob Patterson to talk to me and then months later told my parents that if I were available to accompany them to the Seal Harbor meeting, to bring me along. I eagerly went.

Following the meeting we were invited to tour the absolutely beautiful Rockefeller garden. There Bob Binnewies took me aside. Bob was the number two person on the Acadia National Park staff, but in his spare time he was helping Peggy with details of launching Maine Coast Heritage Trust. He knew that in a few weeks I would be beginning business school, and he asked whether the following summer between my two years of graduate study I might be interested in working for Maine Coast Heritage Trust. Elmer Beal, the first executive director, would begin work in January. I could assist Elmer during the first summer, which was anticipated to be busy and interesting. I did not hesitate in saying yes.

The Maine Coast Heritage Trust office would be located at the new College of the Atlantic in Bar Harbor, which also would be in its first summer of operation in 1971. I arranged to rent a mooring for *Eggemoggin* in Northeast Harbor just off the town dock, and our beloved small yawl would be our home for the summer, providing not only accommodations but transportation to visit island owners on behalf of Maine Coast Heritage Trust. *Eggemoggin* would again sail for conservation.

The creation of Maine Coast Heritage Trust resulted directly from Peggy Rockefeller's and Tom Cabot's increasing concern about the amount of development occurring on islands. Peggy was an avid and accomplished sailor and cruised the coast with David, family, and friends. Summer cottages were appearing on more and more islands, often close to the shore and highly visible, and she feared that the world-class scenery of the Maine coast and its semi-wilderness character would be seriously degraded. Tom Cabot was an even more experienced cruising person, who not only knew the Maine coast very well but, like Peggy and David, had purchased some islands not just for enjoyment but to protect their character. Together Peggy and Tom decided to found a new organization to preserve Maine islands. Most Maine islands were privately owned, and David Strawbridge, a young attorney in whom they had great confidence, was given the task of analyzing what would be the best way for private island owners to preserve the scenic and natural qualities of their islands. The recommendation that came back was to encourage island owners to grant conservation easements.

In a conservation easement the landowner voluntarily deeds away development rights that he or she thinks never should be exercised. A conservation easement is a flexible tool tailored to the characteristics of the particular parcel of land and the needs and wishes of the owners but within the constraints of the criteria of the conservation agency to which it is granted. The restrictions may forbid all development or may allow some development subject to the limitations set forth in the easement. Commercial uses are usually prohibited or limited, and guidelines for tree cutting and vegetation management are typically included. Once executed by the landowner and accepted by the conservation agency that will enforce the provisions, an easement runs in perpetuity regardless of who may own the land in the future.

The conservation agency that first began accepting conservation easements in Maine was Acadia National Park. Shortly thereafter two state agencies began accepting easements as did some towns, and two private nonprofit organizations, The Nature Conservancy and the National Audubon Society, began doing the same. Later, as more and more local land trusts were formed, they too began acquiring conservation easements, as did eventually Maine Coast Heritage Trust itself.

When the conservation easement technique was recommended to Peggy and Tom at the end of the 1960s, it was not a new concept. It had been used sporadically in different parts of the country, primarily to preserve scenic vistas. Early in the twentieth century a number of scenic easements were granted in California, and in the 1930s the National Park Service used such easements to preserve the scenic character of lands along the Blue Ridge and Natchez Trace Parkways in Virginia and Mississippi. Two decades later Wisconsin used easements to protect scenery on the Great River Road along the Mississippi River.

The technique had not caught on widely, though, and was generally little known when Maine Coast Heritage Trust announced its new program of promoting and negotiating conservation easements to be held by Acadia National Park. The Park might thus preserve the scenic and natural qualities of the privately owned islands surrounding Acadia. The extraordinary vistas from the national park itself and from the surrounding waterways were vital to the quality experience enjoyed by visitors to Acadia. The Park's senior management also recognized the importance of protecting the ecosystems of the Acadia archipelago. The preservation of these islands by means of the newly announced Maine Coast Heritage Trust effort was so important to Acadia that the Park's superintendent, John Good, served on the original board of directors.

It is no exaggeration to say that although the conservation easement technique had a long, if little known, history of use in the United States, Maine Coast Heritage Trust in partnership with Acadia National Park lit a spark that caused this particular land conservation technique to become widely popular among conservationists across the country in the coming years. Maine Coast Heritage Trust itself would mature and evolve to become a national leader in land conservation despite staying limited geographically to Maine and primarily the coastal area. That success was due not only to an excellent idea at the outset well suited to the times, the conservation easement, but even more so it was due to an extraordinarily talented and committed group of people.

Peggy Rockefeller set the tone as first president of Maine Coast Heritage Trust's board of directors. Brilliant, hardworking, hugely energetic, dedicated to the mission, demanding of everyone's best efforts yet deeply caring about other people and with a mischievous sense of humor, she was a leader to die for. One of my favorite memories of her was the hot summer day the editor of the *Bar Harbor Times* came to the Maine Coast Heritage Trust office to interview Peggy. He had not previously met her, and when I saw him arrive in a coat and tie, no doubt expecting a formal and stiff Mrs. Rockefeller, I chuckled while we awaited her arrival. This was after she and David had purchased Bartlett Island in Blue Hill Bay and she had become deeply engaged with the herd of cattle that they placed on the island. In a few minutes there was a clump, clump, clump up the stairs, and the odor of cow barn preceded Peggy into the room. Attired in heavy, cow-dung encrusted boots, jeans, and a denim shirt, perspiration dripped off her as she warmly greeted the taken-aback editor.

Tom Cabot as her co-founder and vice president of the board was a hard-driving, highly successful, pragmatic Boston businessman and philanthropist who had tried to explore every nook and cranny of the Maine coast in his yawl *Avelinda*. He once even returned from a walk ashore to find the stern hanging from a rope tied to a spruce tree as the tide dropped. He so loved the Maine islands that he had purchased several in locations stretching from Penobscot Bay to Cutler, and he so respected the people of the Maine coast that a young local man he met on a Jonesport fish pier was hired by him and rose to become president of Cabot Canada before returning in retirement to lobstering in Jonesport.

On the original board too was Harold (Ed) Woodsum, to whom within a couple of years Peggy would turn over the presidency. A Portland native and busy corporate lawyer in that city, Ed had been an all-Ivy end on Yale's football team and looked it. He brought to board meetings the best sense of humor in the state of Maine—and Maine is known for great humor. Ed also brought extraordinary common sense, which was to prove hugely beneficial to board and staff alike in what would turn out to be his thirty years as head of the board of directors. Ed's strong and effective leadership over so many years was an absolutely vital factor in the organization's success.

All of the original board were extraordinary individuals, and over the years as some departed and others arrived, the caliber has been maintained. I remember around 1980, when I was executive director of Maine Coast Heritage Trust, being asked at a national conference what accounted for the track record that by then was nationally known and respected. My answer was that certainly a most important factor was one of the highest-caliber nonprofit boards of directors anywhere. What was really noticeable about this board, though, was not just its caliber but how much fun they had working together.

゜゚゚゚

I was tremendously privileged to join the original staff of Maine Coast Heritage Trust on July 1, 1971, and to begin what would turn out to be a long-term association with this board of directors and with the fine and talented fellow staff members who would be attracted. I had finished my first year of business school at Dartmouth and would assist new executive director Elmer Beal during a busy summer of promoting conservation easements to Maine landowners in the region where Acadia National Park had authority from Congress to acquire them. That region included Hancock County, home of the Mount Desert and Schoodic Districts of the Park. It also included the portion of Knox County south and east of the steamship channel up West Penobscot Bay, wherein lies the Isle au Haut District of Acadia. We focused primarily on owners of islands or portions of islands, but also on owners of key mainland shorefront properties. Elmer and I basically had a sales and marketing job—selling this new-to-Maine idea of voluntarily donating conservation easements.

Maine Coast Heritage Trust was fortunate to attract Elmer as its first executive director. A descendant of a longtime Southwest Harbor lobstering family, he brought to the job an intimate knowledge of the people and culture of the Maine coast. Bright and with a broad education and experience, he had been a music major at Bowdoin, had gone on to two years in the Peace Corps in Latin America, and had a master's degree in anthropology from the University of Texas. He was fun-loving, warm, and dedicated to Maine. I hugely enjoyed working for and with Elmer until he moved on to teaching at College of the Atlantic, managing a small organic farm, and, later, running one of Mount Desert Island's finest restaurants—truly multifaceted and multi-talented!

Elmer was also important to the Trust in helping offset criticism that the organization was a tool of summer people focused on protecting their views and playground. The high profiles of summer residents Peggy Rockefeller and Tom Cabot perhaps made such criticism inevitable in the early years despite the important roles played by native Mainers such as Ed Woodsum. What better than for a young, energetic member of a highly regarded, local fishing family like Elmer to show commitment to the mission by heading the original staff. From the beginning the Trust worked hard to demonstrate its commitment to the broad public good. Little by little over many years it would chip away at the criticisms, expanding its programs over time in ways that broadened the benefits of its efforts, and would become one of Maine's most widely respected conservation organizations.

The first summer of Maine Coast Heritage Trust operations was fun, rewarding, and educational—and successful. Elmer and I spent as little time as possible in our office on the second floor of College of the Atlantic in Bar Harbor and as much time as possible out visiting priority landowners. In those days before personal computers and digital maps Elmer had taped together the nautical charts of the Maine coast. They covered an entire wall. He then had put little paper flags with landowner names on pins, which he inserted through the charts into the bulletin-board backing. The flags were color-coded to distinguish private owners from government owners. That wall was hugely useful to us for many years in prioritizing landowners to be contacted, and it proved a fascinating, eye-catching exhibit for visitors. I often stood reading the flags, thinking about properties associated with them, and deciding whom to contact next and how best to make the approach.

The early successes came quickly as Peggy, Tom, and other board members with island properties led the way in preparing and executing conservation easements. Promoting the use of conservation easements in Maine was akin to marketing any new product, and as Maine Coast Heritage Trust board and staff spread the word, other "early adopters" came to the fore. To my delight several of the island owners of Eggemoggin Reach, my parents included, were among those who very quickly began detailed discussions with us on the Maine Coast Heritage Trust staff and with their attorneys. Protected islands in my own home waters became an early showcase for Maine Coast Heritage Trust. The conversations among the Eggemoggin Reach island owners during the 1960s about ways to ensure perpetuation of the islands' wild and scenic character had laid fertile groundwork. Prior to Maine Coast Heritage Trust's founding, there had not been an evident good way to achieve the desired protection, but after 1970 the conservation easement technique that Maine Coast Heritage Trust was encouraging became the obvious way for island owners to preserve their islands' natural qualities permanently yet continue the private ownership.

Another of Maine Coast Heritage Trust's original board members was my Brooklin neighbor Alan Bemis. He owned a little island off his house, and his best friend owned two just beyond. Like Peggy and Tom he too was avid about cruising along the Maine coast, which he did for many years in his renowned and lovely, dark red Herreshoff-designed and -built yawl *Cirrus*. In those first years of Maine Coast Heritage Trust, Alan was commodore of the Cruising Club of America, a post which enhanced his access to and credibility both with many island owners and with others who loved the Maine coast and were willing to help support conservation efforts. Gregarious and a beloved master at telling downeast stories, Alan was tireless in beating the conservation drum. On one or two occasions I joined him on *Cirrus* to go call on an island owner, and his engineering my admission to the Cruising Club of America at that time helped establish my own credibility with a number of key landowners. You sell yourself, then you sell the product. That essentially was our task and our *modus operandi* in promoting conservation easements.

Alan Bemis by dint of personality and hard sailing made his classic yawl *Cirrus* into a local icon, well-known as belonging to an ardent enthusiast for preserving the Maine coast. *Cirrus*'s connection to the work of Maine Coast Heritage Trust was to continue after he sold her to a great friend of both his and mine, the late Sue Drew. Alan, I, and others over literally decades talked to Sue about her Harriman Point property jutting into Blue Hill Bay. Our shared admiration for the boat was one of many bonds that linked us.

Sue was hugely generous in allowing local residents to enjoy Harriman Point, which is easy of access by foot from the public road but provides an experience almost like being on an undeveloped island. Conversations about what are the most important properties in Brooklin to preserve almost always zeroed in on Harriman Point. Sue, however, for understandable personal reasons avoided firm commitments as to what she might do, but upon her passing away just a few years ago, most in the local community and Maine Coast Heritage Trust were thrilled to learn that she had bequeathed her lovely Blue Hill Bay peninsula to the Trust as a preserve for public enjoyment. The town was so pleased that the town meeting voted to approve allowing a small, nearby town-owned parcel to be used for visitor parking, and the local Baptist church permitted a trail across land that it owns to facilitate access from the parking lot. By the time of Sue's death Maine Coast Heritage Trust, by then an owner of many preserves, had evolved far beyond its narrow original mission of just promoting and negotiating conservation easements to be held and enforced by other entities.

During the first summer I frequently used my own little yawl *Eggemoggin* to call on island owners. In those first years of Maine Coast Heritage Trust I had a lot of fun doing that and some entertaining incidents. One afternoon I arrived at an island off Stonington to find the owning couple's wife swimming a few yards off the float and her husband gone to Stonington for supplies. I had been encouraged to stop by, so I circled the swimming woman and chatted with her for awhile. Suddenly it dawned on me, given the frigidity of the ocean water in Maine, that she must be extraordinarily hardy. I commented, "I certainly admire your being able to stay in this cold water so long."

Her reply: "What else can I do? I don't have any clothes on!" *Eggemoggin* was relatively slow under power, and it took me a painfully long time to make my exit.

I had only worked for Maine Coast Heritage Trust for a couple of weeks when I was asked if I would stay on through the winter and not return for my second year of business school. I was sorely tempted to agree and postpone finishing my M.B.A. degree, because I was thrilled with my Maine Coast Heritage Trust work and so much loved being in Maine. Fortunately, over the telephone the Tuck School dean offered wise counsel. He encouraged me to realize that it would be much easier for me in the long run to stay on track and finish what I was already halfway to completing. "Ask if you can return full-time in May," he advised. Maine Coast Heritage Trust agreed to that plan, and in May 1972, immediately following my last exam and without waiting for graduation, Judy and I were on the road from New Hampshire back to Maine, accompanied by our five-month-old daughter Kristin.

We had bought a house in Pretty Marsh on the west side of Mount Desert Island just before we left the previous fall. We now had a home on shore. *Eggemoggin* would not again be our summer home but remained available for fun and Maine Coast Heritage Trust island trips. Not a small reason for my excitement at the prospect of full-time work for Maine Coast Heritage Trust was the long sailing season that I would have.

☙

By the second summer of operations, Maine Coast Heritage Trust had expanded its geographic range. Acadia National Park's lacking authority to accept conservation easements outside of Hancock County and part of Knox County severely restricted our initial activity, but the State of Maine through two of its agencies, the Department of Inland Fisheries and Wildlife and the then Department of Parks and Recreation, decided to begin accepting easements. That enabled us to extend Maine Coast Heritage Trust promotional efforts the length of the Maine coast and even, to some degree, inland. I recall working with a landowner at that time all the way up on a pond near Moosehead Lake.

We also by the second summer had faster water transport available. Initially, Maine Coast Heritage Trust had acquired an old lobsterboat for water transport, which Elmer Beal primarily used. By the second year that was gone, and we had an Aquasport, an open, center-console, outboard-powered boat which could cruise at over 20 knots. Both Elmer and I used it, and for me it was my first experience of regularly traveling Maine coastal waters at greater than sailboat speed. Distances shrank disconcertingly. North Haven was no longer a day's sail away but rather not much over an hour. Some of the coast's romance was lost, but I could not argue with the efficiency when being paid to produce conservation results.

I also used Maine Coast Heritage Trust's Aquasport to explore and expand my knowledge of the coast, especially of places where I hesitated to take a sailboat with a small engine and deep keel. One of the first places I poked into in the Aquasport was The Basin on Vinalhaven's western shore with its rock-strewn, narrow entrance sluiced by racing current except at slack water. Years later other Maine Coast Heritage Trust staff members would achieve major conservation success in protecting much of this unique and lovely waterbody's shoreline.

The process of promoting and facilitating conservation easements was relatively straightforward. We would identify key owners of island properties and then decide how to make the initial contact. If a board member knew a property owner, the board member might make the first contact, perhaps give a brief introduction to what Maine Coast Heritage Trust was doing, and ask if a Maine Coast Heritage Trust staff person—Elmer or me—would be welcome to make a call. In other cases, Elmer or I would simply make the first contact directly by letter and telephone. We would try to schedule an appointment, although in the case of island owners living on their islands during unscheduled summer days, we might find ourselves encouraged to just stop by when we could. When we sat down with property owners, we explained all the technicalities about conservation easements and left explanatory materials.

Once a property owner was ready to consider a conservation

easement seriously, the next step would usually be for us to prepare a draft conservation easement, which the landowner could take to his or her attorney. We also laid the groundwork with the agency chosen to accept the easement, whether Acadia National Park or one of the two state agencies. Early on we also added the alternatives of The Nature Conservancy and the National Audubon Society. At that time the Maine statute did not provide for nonprofit organizations to hold conservation easements. It was some years before the statute would be amended to permit that, but under common law nonprofit conservation organizations could hold "easements appurtenant." That required their owning an abutting piece of land or at least one very close in line of sight. There often was the possibility of a landowner who wanted to grant a conservation easement to a nonprofit organization rather than a government agency gifting a small piece of land to be the necessary anchor parcel.

The Nature Conservancy with its Maine Chapter was a very important partner organization for Maine Coast Heritage Trust from the latter's beginning. Since the Turtle Island acquisition by The Nature Conservancy in 1963, it had slowly added to its holdings of islands as preserves. By deciding to also hold easements appurtenant on privately owned property, it expanded its tool kit of conservation techniques. Its Maine Chapter at the time had one staff person, a wonderful older man named Charles Bradford, who earlier in his career had gained respect in charge of the state park system. I used to laugh at this environmental leader's driving around Maine in the years immediately following the heightened environmental consciousness of Earth Day in one of those big, fuel-guzzling station wagons with fake wood trim. Time went by; I mellowed; my children and dogs multiplied; and for years I loved driving a whole series of those comfy but environmentally questionable vehicles.

Probably surprising-seeming now, The Nature Conservancy's Maine Chapter and Maine Coast Heritage Trust even discussed possible merger during the 1970s. Both were active in coastal conservation; the Conservancy had a national presence and reputation; Maine Coast Heritage Trust had the best fund-raising capabilities in Maine at the time thanks to the resources and contacts of the founders. Putting the two efforts together in Maine seemed worth considering. Obviously, it never happened. The Nature Conservancy became ever more science-driven in its programs, pushed in that direction by its powerful and effective head scientist at national headquarters in Virginia, Bob Jenkins. Maine Coast Heritage Trust continued to apply much broader—and over time increasingly broad—criteria including, in addition to ecological significance, the public benefits of scenic preservation, protecting community culture and natural resource–based job sources, and enhancing outdoor recreation opportunities. It also kept its primary area of focus close to the coast as The Nature Conservancy increasingly turned its activity inland. Both programs were to grow drastically in terms of staffing and budgets.

Adding nonprofits to the list of entities willing to hold conservation easements was important because some landowners balked at dealing with government agencies. Most extreme was the landowner who refused to deal with Acadia National Park because it was a federal agency. He was furious with the federal government due to the Vietnam War, which was still raging. Fortunately, he did not hold against me my Navy time off Vietnam. Others simply mistrusted government. In contrast, some like Tom Cabot believed that only the federal government was a reliable holder of conservation easements for the long run. It was remote from local politics, did not depend for survival on the vagaries of fundraising, and had all the resources of the U.S. Department of Justice to bring to bear, if necessary, to enforce conservation easement restrictions. Offering a choice of holders for easements proved very helpful to Maine Coast Heritage Trust progress.

Elmer did a fine job as Maine Coast Heritage Trust's first executive director in launching Maine Coast Heritage Trust, but he was intrigued by teaching and grabbed an opportunity to join the growing College of the Atlantic faculty in Maine Coast Heritage Trust's second year. I was sorry to see Elmer depart but happy that Bob Binnewies, who knew the organization well from having helped with early administrative details, took a leave of absence from the National Park Service to replace Elmer. Bob was a westerner like so many National Park Service personnel. He had been at Acadia long enough, though, to know at least the Acadia portion of Maine well, and he was dedicated to conserving its extraordinary natural qualities. He and I enjoyed working together, our desks only feet apart, as we strove to build relationships with more and more property owners and thereby expand the number of islands and mainland shorefront properties protected by conservation easements. During the summers we called on property owners in Maine. So many key property owners lived out of state in the winters, however, that we traveled frequently, setting up appointments in Boston, New York, Philadelphia, Washington, and points in between. At that time Maine landowners whose primary residences were elsewhere were heavily concentrated in the East, especially the Northeast. That is less true today.

By 1974 the scope of Maine Coast Heritage Trust operations was such that we began to consider opening a second office in southern Maine to give us easier access to landowners there and to establish a presence near the power centers of Portland and the state capital of Augusta. Initially, I agreed to move and open a southern Maine office, but my bonds to my own home landscape in Hancock County and, to be honest, the terrific sailing that it afforded me caused me to change my mind. I opted not to make a permanent move southward. That led us to offer the job of opening a second office to a brilliant young woman whose love for Maine was so deep that she had sought us out.

The years of the early 1970s followed closely upon the first Earth Day in April 1970, and the idealism remained strong. Many of our generation wanted to find work opportunities in environmental protection. At Maine Coast Heritage Trust we received frequent letters inquiring about job possibilities. We had no job openings, and we so responded to inquiries. In the fall or winter of 1973–74, however, I opened one of these letters of inquiry, and the writer's passion for the Maine coast was so superbly articulated that I passed it over to Bob saying that we should meet the person. She was only a half mile away in an entry-level, post-college job at the Maine Sea Coast Mission. Janet Milne was from Connecticut but had spent summers at her family's cottage on Deer Isle. Bob and I were so impressed upon meeting her that we offered her some part-time work calling on Maine landowners in southern New England. Summer employment was soon offered, followed by our asking her to join the regular Maine Coast Heritage Trust staff and open the southern Maine office.

Janet was to play a major role in the evolution of Maine Coast Heritage Trust in regard to its standing in Maine and nationally. She was to become a highly valued colleague as well as close personal friend. For the short run, though, I was making plans to leave Maine Coast Heritage Trust to try new challenges. After helping Janet get off to an excellent start with Maine Coast Heritage Trust and open the new Brunswick office in the fall of 1974, I departed for what turned out to be only about a year and a half.

Benefits of Land Conservation—Endlessly Broad and Increasingly Understood
As described in this book my professional engagement with land conservation began in 1971 with the launching of the game-changing Acadia National Park/Maine Coast Heritage Trust conservation easement program to protect the scenic and natural qualities of Maine's coastal islands. Subsequent decades of participating in and observing land conservation efforts in Maine and across the nation have led me to understand the following as critical benefits of the type of land conservation work recorded herein:
Preserving beautiful scenery and natural wildness;
Preserving habitat for flora and fauna;
Preserving public access to land and water for outdoor recreation;
Protecting water quality, fresh and salt, with vegetative buffers;
Protecting working forests and farms;
Protecting working waterfronts;
Preserving areas for scientific research and for education;
Guiding where development goes;
Complementing government land use regulations;
Maintaining "Quality of Place";
Enhancing sense of community, maintaining traditions, and building community pride;
Enhancing resilience of ecosystems to the warming climate.

6

HURRICANE

When I left the Maine Coast Heritage Trust staff in the fall of 1974, I was drawn away by a desire both to try something new professionally and to undertake another sailing adventure. By the time two more years had passed, I would be back at Maine Coast Heritage Trust after having been engaged in two separate efforts related to trying to protect the environment and help Maine people. I would have a wonderful family sailing adventure followed by surviving unexpected severe turbulence—hurricanes both literally and figuratively.

Passion for the sea and the coastal zone led to a project with the Boston-based New England Natural Resources Center analyzing how well equipped the five coastal New England states were to cope with the onshore impacts of offshore oil development. For the second time—and there would be a third time—Hank Foster, then still chairing the New England Natural Resources Center board, opened an opportunity for me. At that time there was ongoing exploration for oil off New England and fear that onshore impacts of a large find could be massive. I spent time meeting with knowledgeable people in Maine, New Hampshire, Massachusetts, Rhode Island, and Connecticut and examined the existing land use laws in each. I wrote and the New England Natural Resources Center published a booklet on my findings and recommendations. That led to a job offer from the State of Maine to work on offshore oil issues. I declined because of sailing plans, one of the times when addiction to sailing and boats interfered with professional opportunities.

By 1974 Judy and I had owned *Eggemoggin* for four years. I was ready to sell the little yawl and buy a boat with more oceangoing capability. Now that Kristin was two years old and growing fast, more space when cruising would be nice. I thought I remained dedicated to wooden boats despite the fact that good fiberglass cruising and racing sailboats had been proving their worth for over fifteen years. I had been looking at used wooden boats in the 40-foot range over several months when my friend Bob Hinckley of the Hinckley Company telephoned one morning.

Bob is a masterful salesman, and he got right to the point. One of the highly acclaimed—and still popular to this day—Hinckley Bermuda 40 keel/centerboard yawls was coming on the market. The boat had become too much for the aging owner to handle. He had called Bob and told Bob a price that he wanted that was significantly below market value. Here was an opportunity that seemed to fit my criteria—except for the fiberglass construction. Said Bob on the phone, "Sail a nice fiberglass boat for forty-five minutes, and you will forget that she is fiberglass." Bob was convincing enough that I went to look at this Bermuda 40 where it lay on its mooring in the Damariscotta River.

The delightful elderly gentleman who owned her was literally a singlehander, having lost an arm in a plane crash. I bought her with the agreement that the seller might have one last cruise in her to Grand Manan, then leave her at the Hinckley yard in Southwest Harbor for survey. A couple of weeks later she was there, and the yard crew told me that when the owner had left her, he had been in tears, hating to say good-bye to his beloved yawl. That owner, whose property on the Damariscotta River was truly a gem, later worked with Maine Coast Heritage Trust to grant a conservation easement. He and I clearly had shared interests. I felt honored to have acquired his yawl, which we also named *Eggemoggin*. I began planning for the following year a summer devoted to family and cruising.

In mid-June 1975 with three others in crew we let go *Eggemoggin*'s mooring bound nonstop for Halifax, where Judy and Kristin joined me and from where the others returned home. A morning or two later we were anchored in a cove on the outer Nova Scotia coast on a gray, foggy morning typical of June. About 7:30 there was a knock on the hull, and I stuck my head up the companionway to find a lobsterboat alongside. The fisherman simply wanted to welcome us, saying that we were the first American yacht of the season, and he asked if we needed anything. I was astounded and could not picture a Maine counterpart of his reaching out to a visiting sailboat in such an open manner. I knew how extraordinarily hospitable Nova Scotians could be, though, from prior visits to Halifax after Marblehead to Halifax Races and during a week in port for repairs by the Canadian Navy following our destroyer's cracking a hull weld in mid-Atlantic. "Get to Halifax before you sink," the admiral had ordered. The people of Nova Scotia turn to for visitors in a way that is a bit foreign to me after a life of experience with New England reserve, but it is wonderful and memorable.

After four days working our way east from Halifax including an absolutely frigid ocean swim to clear a jibsheet fouled in the propeller, we entered the Bras d'Or Lakes through St. Peter's Canal. Totally enclosed by Cape Breton Island except for narrow entrances on the eastern and western sides of the island, the lakes offer much warmer waters and much more sunshine than outside as well as protected sailing waters and lovely scenery. I had briefly visited and sailed in the lakes four years earlier when Maine Coast Heritage Trust board member Alan Bemis, a pilot, asked me to accompany him in his single-engine aircraft. He had bought property on the lakes some years earlier, land which he later gave to the Nature Conservancy of Canada. We landed in his hayfield and spent a cold, rainy weekend on the heavy, double-ended Norwegian cutter *Direction*, which had gained fame for carrying artist Rockwell Kent on a voyage to Greenland and ultimate shipwreck. Resurrected, *Direction* came into the ownership of Carl and Margaret Vilas and gave them many happy years. For me it was a privilege to spend a weekend aboard with them and Alan, and my appetite for more cruising in the Bras d'Or Lakes was whetted. Hence, our arrival in *Eggemoggin*.

The lakes were ideal for three weeks of cruising with our three-year-old Kristin. In her first summers she had grown used to naps in a hammock swinging from the overhead of the first *Eggemoggin*. Now she graduated to napping on the cockpit sole—very safe as long as we avoided stepping on her. Every day brought family fun, and a couple of days each week we anchored off an island near Baddeck, the main town on the Lakes, because the island had a day camp for small children. We were eager for Kristin to have socialization time with other

children. We would row her ashore on those mornings and turn her
over to the camp staff for a few hours of play. We sailed; we hiked; we
swam; we scooped up oysters in the shallows. One beach was so steep
that we could run down it and dive into the water. There we brought
our shallow-draft yawl right into shore and put the bow on the beach,
keeping the boat under control with a stern anchor.

What particularly delighted me in the Bras d'Or Lakes were the
bald eagles. Maine had suffered a catastrophic decline in eagles, and we
simply did not see eagles when on the water in Maine. I watched them
in fascination, never guessing that Maine's eagle population would
recover and that by the early 1990s I would be personally involved in
protecting eagle nesting habitat on Maine coastal islands.

With a young child aboard we forewent jumping across Cabot
Strait to Newfoundland, but we did venture out of the Lakes to the east
and sailed up the eastern Cape Breton shore to Ingonish. Extraordinary
Scottish music drifting down a steep wooded hillside to our anchorage enticed us to explore ashore. We found ourselves at an absolutely
delightful outdoor evening concert at a school of highland arts.

Too soon this special family time afloat came to an end, and what
I could not know was that future family times would be very different.
Friends had picked up our car where Judy had left it in Halifax. They
delivered it to Cape Breton and joined the crew. Following a few days
with all of us on board together Judy and Kristin departed for home in
the car while the three of us remaining headed to sea into an evening
fog on a straight shot to Halifax. Changing crew there *Eggemoggin* again
headed out to sea, bound for Mount Desert Island and home waters.

Just before we left the dock in Halifax, I telephoned the Halifax airport
weather bureau and learned of a tropical system off North Carolina. I
was told that it was moving slowly and would bend to the east, posing
no threat to us on our projected track southwestward from Halifax to
the southwest tip of Nova Scotia at Cape Sable, then northwest across
the Gulf of Maine to Northeast Harbor. As a precaution, though, I was

advised to stay abreast of weather forecasts. The weather bureau did expect some showers two days later resulting from a low-pressure system moving eastward across Quebec.

In sparkling sunshine we departed Halifax in late afternoon, steering to the south-southwest and sailing hard on the starboard tack. The fresh west-to-southwest winds moderated through the night, and by breakfast time we were heading west under power through calm seas. We consistently encountered difficulty obtaining good weather forecasts when at sea off Nova Scotia, but we did hear a routine commercial broadcast that morning that indicated nothing unusual. The sky was our only other source of weather information, for our barometer was broken. A high, thin but not threatening overcast gradually thickened through the day. In late afternoon a light southeast wind began to fill in, and when we were convinced that it would last, we turned off the engine and set the spinnaker.

After that morning's forecast I thought little more about the weather until suppertime, when a trawler passed close by us traveling rapidly toward Lunenburg. As she passed our stern, a man stepped from the wheelhouse to shout something. Only our youngest crew member, a thirteen-year-old, understood anything of the fisherman's words. He thought he had heard the word "storm." We immediately turned on the radio but could only get a New Brunswick forecast. The next day was to bring heavy rain and strong northeast winds, which although wet would be perfect for a fast reach across the Bay of Fundy. I supposed this to be the low-pressure system from Quebec that the Halifax weather bureau had mentioned, but to be safe we monitored 2182 KHZ, the emergency frequency, for a time. On 2182 we heard occasional instructions to switch to another frequency for a weather message, but our set lacked that frequency. We did, however, find aviation weather for the United States east coast, and airports from Bangor to Annapolis were reporting perfect weather.

The southeast wind freshened through the evening hours. At midnight, sailing under spinnaker through thick fog and with unreliable fixes from our radio direction finder, we thought it prudent to drop the spinnaker and unroll our roller-furling genoa. Shortly before dawn the wind freshened some more. In the early light and with the wind well aft, estimating wind speed was difficult, but rolling up the genoa put the boat under easy control. For the next hour while others sailed I slept fitfully, once calling up to the helmsman to ask if there seemed any danger of rolling the main boom into a wave top. The answer was negative. Heavy rain beating on the deck forecast a wet morning on watch.

Shortly after six o'clock, asleep again, I was brought instantly to my feet by a crash on deck. A wave had slewed the boat so that the wind caught the mainsail on its leeward side, the vang holding down the boom broke, and only the preventer line from boom end to bow cleat, which was rigged to stop an accidental jibe, kept the boom from slamming across the boat.

I reached for my foulweather gear only to realize that the wind was increasing by the second in the wet, gray morning. There was no time for foulweather gear, but I did slip on a safety harness before I and another crew member made our way forward to drop the mainsail. As soon as it was secured, we dropped the mizzen and gave the helmsman the peace of mind of knowing that the dancing mizzenmast would not crash down on him.

Two of us again made our way forward, this time to set the storm jib. Work on the foredeck could only be accomplished by lying absolutely flat with elbows and legs spread. Communicating could only be done by yelling or hand signals. Time and again waves towered over the foredeck, and we would hang on for an expected avalanche of water. Each time, though, *Eggemoggin* surprised us by rising and letting the walls of water pass harmlessly beneath her.

While those of us on deck were changing sails, those below had monitored the early-morning radio reports. Immediately, word came over that the center of what was now called Hurricane Blanche was 60 miles due south of our position headed due north at 18 knots. That report was a shock, especially because worse conditions were clearly still to come. Winds close to the center were reported at 60 knots gusting to 70 to 80. We had estimated the wind to be in that range prior to hearing the radio, although when the wind is blowing that hard, estimates of wind speed are little better than guesses. The southeast winds confirmed that we were in the dangerous quadrant of the storm, where the wind speeds we were encountering were a combination of the speed of the wind circulating around the storm center and the speed of the forward motion of the storm. Traveling fast with the wind on our port quarter, we were at least headed for the hurricane's so-called safe quadrant.

The seas throughout the morning remained very confused and steep, and they came from all directions. The worst of them we estimated to be 15 to 20 feet high. What made the seas so confused at our location south of Cape Sable, the southwest corner of Nova Scotia, was that the southeast wind reached hurricane force just shortly before the current ebbing to the southeast out of the Bay of Fundy reached maximum strength. Then soon after the wind shifted to the northwest following passage of the eye in mid-morning, the current also switched to again run counter to the wind. It was the ugliness of the seas that persuaded me to keep the boat moving under storm jib rather than try to lie ahull or run under bare poles. In those seas I thought that we needed as much steering control as possible. Under the storm jib we were almost becalmed in the troughs, then hit hard on the crests, but the boat kept moving with the speedometer registering up to 8 knots.

As the storm center bore down on us, we only once filled the cockpit with water as one wave threw the boat down on its side before another wave going the other way broke over the cockpit coaming. Shortly thereafter, as I was steering, *Eggemoggin* heeled sharply to port, her rail again going under as water came almost to the top of the coaming. At the same time a wave reared up to port. There on the slope of the wave, seemingly where I could put my hand out to touch them, were three slicing dorsal fins. The boat rolled to the other side, and I never saw them again. I thought sharks at the time, but dolphins seem more likely. Before mid-morning the wind began to shift noticeably more easterly, then into the northeast. By this time the heavy rain had given way to fog and low, scudding overcast. As the wind backed, we steered more and more southerly, then to the east of south, to keep it behind us. Moderating winds and occasional glimpses of sun through streaked, yellow-gray clouds accompanied the wind shift. When the wind settled into the northwest, we began to experience periods of blue sky to the northwest alternating with the fog and heavy overcast. The wind again increased, blowing as hard from the northwest as it had from the southeast. We felt confident that the 180-degree wind shift had to mean that the storm center had passed, yet radio reports continued to place it south of us. We remained apprehensive that we might still not have seen the worst, but finally the weather forecasters updated the storm's position, putting it past us.

About noon the wind abated again. We set the storm trysail in addition to the storm jib and headed as much to the southwest and toward New England as the seas would allow. A few slammed the windward side hard, and sheets of spray across the boat indicated the upper limit of a comfortable course. Soon wind and seas began to drop off as rapidly as they had increased six hours earlier. The full mainsail replaced the storm trysail, and under mainsail and storm jib we finally were able to head northwesterly toward Mount Desert Island in southwesterly winds of about 25 knots.

Home again, I prepared to shift gears at summer's end. Halsey Smith, a former Portland bank president and a Maine Coast Heritage Trust board member, headed the Center for Research and Advanced Study at what was then the University of Maine at Portland-Gorham, later renamed the University of Southern Maine. I was to join the Project New Enterprise team at the Center assisting new small Maine businesses with growth potential. I was paid by a funding source interested in both Maine conservation and economic development. Maine Coast Heritage Trust had given serious thought in the first years to trying to help small businesses but decided that for one tiny nonprofit conservation organization it would be too much of a square peg in a round hole.

Halsey welcomed me warmly to his project. Judy was expecting our second child and gave birth to Thor in November. She elected to stay at home on Mount Desert while I spent most of each week in Portland, coming home for long weekends. Soon I was engaged with Maine's two original salmon aquaculture operations, some of Maine's wood-turning and -shaping businesses, a raiser of meat rabbits, and a producer of frozen baked stuffed potatoes. I even remember meeting with what had to be a very early—this was 1975–76—maker of modern wind turbine blades, which were of wood. This was intriguing and different work for a while but not playing to my strongest interests.

As it turned out, I was at the Center only until spring. Bob Binnewies, still executive director of Maine Coast Heritage Trust, had decided to return to the National Park Service. Would I please return to the Maine Coast Heritage Trust staff and take over from him? I was ecstatic to say good-bye to my life of commuting to Portland and return to Mount Desert Island full-time. I much looked forward to my first summer as Maine Coast Heritage Trust's executive director and did not foresee the trauma that would darken it.

7
AT THE HELM OF
MAINE COAST HERITAGE TRUST

For the following six years beginning that spring of 1976 I served as executive director of Maine Coast Heritage Trust. Those six years would be highly eventful for the family and me personally, for the organization, and for land conservation nationally. Through the ups and downs of those years I continued active summertime sailing in Maine and made time to race *Eggemoggin* and a successor of the same name in two consecutive Marion, Massachusetts, to Bermuda Races.

On my return to Maine Coast Heritage Trust, Janet Milne became my associate director. She still ran Maine Coast Heritage Trust's southern Maine office and had earned immense respect for her capabilities and effectiveness. Together we eagerly began developing plans for increasing the pace of protecting more land and, equally importantly, enhancing public understanding of and support for land conservation efforts. Promoting and negotiating conservation easements remained the primary thrust of Maine Coast Heritage Trust, but we increasingly saw the need to demonstrate why it was publicly beneficial to conserve the scenic, ecological, and cultural qualities of land.

In the early years of Maine Coast Heritage Trust there had been some negative press to the effect that the goal was to protect the pretty views from the shorefront houses of the wealthy. It was essential to counter that perception. In Massachusetts conservation restrictions, as they were called there, required approval of the municipal governing body. That was not the case in Maine, and we did not want to see that layer of complexity added to completing conservation easements. In Maine that might be particularly problematic, for the majority of grantors of conservation easements at the time were summer residents. Requiring town government approval might engender an "us and them" dialogue that we did not care to have. Nonetheless, we wanted to encourage conceptual support from the public and from town officials to the extent that we could. I give Janet credit for focusing Maine Coast Heritage Trust on this issue and leading the internal effort to explain to the Maine Coast Heritage Trust board of directors why it was so important.

We took advantage of opportunities to speak about the Maine Coast Heritage Trust program as often as we could. Rotary Clubs were a particular venue for our presentations. Under Janet's leadership we launched a project that was to prove a forerunner of similar efforts around the nation later and continuing to this day—tying land conservation to public economic benefit. Maine Coast Heritage Trust collaborated with the Maine Association of Conservation Commissions, which was led by the exceptionally dedicated Tad Dow, and with the University of Maine. We had helpful advice too from Bob Lemire, who had made a name for himself promoting open space conservation and carefully planned limited development in Lincoln, Massachusetts. Bob Doucette, an economist from the University, worked with us to develop an economic model for comparing the fiscal impacts on a town's budget of conserving open space versus having the same land's being subdivided for housing. Maine Coast Heritage Trust published the model with appropriate explanation and blank worksheets in a hefty book.

In multiple locations along the coast we sponsored well-publicized workshops aimed at selectmen, planning board officials, and conservation commissioners. These evening workshops proved effective ways to demonstrate that conserving open space often was far less a burden on a town's budget than providing the municipal services required for housing subdivisions. Equally importantly, the workshops provided a relaxed and focused environment in which to discuss what Maine Coast Heritage Trust was trying to accomplish and to hear and talk about concerns. In fact, given the limitations of our economic model and the wide array of variables that real situations presented, the greatest benefit of these evenings no doubt was the opportunity to become personally acquainted with more town officials, to show that we respected and were influenced by their viewpoints and were doing our best to do conservation work in ways that benefited their communities.

Over the years I have noticed how much the wheel turns in land conservation as in so many other endeavors. Years after we had presented our economic model to town officials and long after I had moved on from being Maine Coast Heritage Trust's executive director, I observed with interest how Maine Coast Heritage Trust hired a consultant to look at the economic impacts in several towns of what Maine Coast Heritage Trust had accomplished, and I saw similar studies from elsewhere. Such studies continue, and the effort to link land conservation with economic benefit to the public steadily increases.

When I returned to Maine Coast Heritage Trust in the spring of 1976, Acadia National Park was once again seeking public approval of a draft Master Plan. This was my second involvement in what in those years seemed an endless series of failing efforts, which did not finally lead to a Master Plan approved by Congress until 1986. The 1972 and 1976 presentations of draft Master Plans were an eye-opener for me in how a skilled opponent can torpedo well-intentioned efforts. The late Jim Haskell, whose intellectual capabilities were evidenced by his having a received a graduate degree from the Harvard School of Design, was at that time executive director of the Hancock County Planning Commission.

On a podium Jim could fan local biases against the federal government—attitudes emanating from New England's long tradition of local control—with the oratorical skill and techniques of an evangelical preacher. In 1972 Acadia National Park had proposed the acquisition of 900-acre Marshall Island, which lies just east of the Isle au Haut District of the Park, for wilderness camping. Jim was married into the family that owned the portion of Marshall that includes its famed and popular Sand Cove, and Jim successfully fought that proposal with particular skill and fervor. It would be many years later before Marshall Island finally was conserved in its entirety thanks to the outstanding work of Maine Coast Heritage Trust's David MacDonald and placed in the ownership of Maine Coast Heritage Trust itself.

By 1976 both Janet and I had come to know Jim personally and, in fact, had dinner with him to discuss the Master Plan effort and our own Maine Coast Heritage Trust conservation easement program. In these one-on-one sessions with Jim I enjoyed him and found him knowledgeable about land conservation techniques, seemingly supportive of our work, and very rational. Then in public meetings he would return to his tirades against Acadia National Park, and we found ourselves on opposite sides of very public controversies. If any one individual stalled the Master Plan efforts of those years, it was Jim. I have always wondered whether the National Park Service would have succeeded in having Congress approve a Master Plan for Acadia years earlier if Jim had not been on the scene.

The fanning of feelings against the federal government deepened local concerns about the conservation easements being acquired by Acadia National Park. Any federal say in regard to local lands was unwelcome in some quarters, even if private property owners, exercising their free rights as landowners, voluntarily placed their lands under such conservation easements. Park Service officials had been becoming increasingly wary of local backlash for several years.

About 1973 the relatively new Acadia National Park superintendent at the time had left Bob Binnewies, then Maine Coast Heritage Trust executive director, and me in a state of shock when he declined to accept an offered conservation easement over the southern end of Newbury Neck in Surry. I well remember the three of us walking over the property and hearing the superintendent say that because Newbury Neck was mainland and not an island, he thought it would be best to decline the easement offer. At that time the Park had legal authority to acquire conservation easements on the mainland in Hancock County. The end of Newbury Neck, which juts into Blue Hill Bay between the two magnificent islands Bartlett and Long, both later protected, not only appeared to be part of the beautiful island landscape when viewed from down the bay but was highly visible from many vantage points within the Park. Its scenic importance was striking.

This backing away by Acadia National Park from using legal authority which it possessed, first evidenced that day walking along the Newbury Neck shore, had by 1976 led to drafting of criteria that conservation easements to be held by the Park must meet. We at Maine Coast Heritage Trust helped refine the criteria, but we were dismayed that the Park was willing to leave completely to other conservation organizations and agencies the conserving of mainland properties—even when such properties were highly significant to the natural integrity of the immediate environs of Acadia National Park and the experiences enjoyed by visitors to the Park and on the public waters of the bays. We saw the benefits of criteria, but we hated to see Park Service officials at Acadia and at the regional National Park Service office willingly yield existing authority. When the Master Plan finally passed Congress, gone was the authority to hold mainland easements except close to the Schoodic District of Acadia. Gone too under separate legislation for Isle au Haut was the authority to hold conservation easements within the town of Isle au Haut even though the Park owns half the big island of Isle au Haut and the smaller neighboring islands within the town limits are very much part of the scenery, the enjoyment of which is so much part of the visitor experience there. In the case of Isle au Haut, Jim Haskell had done a particularly good job of stoking local fears about the federal government.

My attention to Acadia National Park Master Plan issues during the first summer back at Maine Coast Heritage Trust was cut short by Judy's sudden passing away in August. Grieved and stunned, I had two small children to care for. My priorities went heavily to them. For a time I shortened my working hours, and I never completely regained as executive director the focus and enthusiasm with which I had returned to Maine Coast Heritage Trust.

Getting a new grip on the lives of my children and myself forced me to rely more than I had anticipated on other staff members' abilities and dedication. Janet brought great credit to the organization for two more years until she departed for law school and a distinguished career in that arena. One of Maine Coast Heritage Trust's best-known accomplishments during this period was the writing and publishing of *The Landowner's Options* under a contract with the Maine State Planning Office. This was totally Janet's project except to the extent that I helped her with editing, and the product was so good that it was copied in several other states and updated several times in Maine. It was the first concise, written summary of the land conservation techniques available to a landowner, how they worked, and what were income, estate, and property tax consequences. At the time, this booklet was a major contribution to the land conservation field. The other full-time member of our small Maine Coast Heritage Trust management team, someone who also worked hard to make the organization effective and my life easier, was Roberta Parritt. Commuting from her home in Steuben just across the county line in Washington County, she not only provided talent and able administrative assistance but also lifelong knowledge and understanding of coastal Maine communities. We needed the perspective of a person whose local roots on the Maine coast stretched back generations. Years later I was delighted when, after a long time in Boston, Roberta reappeared on the Maine coast with her husband, retiring to the Schoodic Peninsula and becoming very much engaged in their adopted community of Winter Harbor.

When Janet departed, we hired Earl Ireland to replace her. Earl had been executive director of the Washington Hancock Community Action Program, a major social service agency for the two easternmost Maine counties. He was well liked and respected in the communities of eastern Maine, and he led us to one of the milestone land projects of Maine Coast Heritage Trust's first decade.

Throughout the early years Maine Coast Heritage Trust stuck to its role as a middleman—promoting land conservation to landowners and arranging conservation solutions, usually conservation easements, with other nonprofit conservation organizations such as National Audubon and The Nature Conservancy, and with government agencies such as Acadia National Park, the Maine Bureau of Parks and Recreation, and the Maine Department of Inland Fisheries and Wildlife. The Maine Coast Heritage Trust board of directors stuck to its determination to hold no real estate interests. Even though co-founder Tom Cabot's original expectation that Maine Coast Heritage Trust could be shut down within five years, having accomplished what it would be possible to accomplish with willing landowners, was proving wrong, he and probably other board members continued to view Maine Coast Heritage Trust as a temporary program. They wanted no responsibilities in perpetuity.

Even raising money for land projects was not something that Maine Coast Heritage Trust then did. We relied totally on landowners' generous willingness either to voluntarily restrict and guide the future use of their land through conservation easements or to donate the land to a conservation entity. We had, however, been encouraged to begin a fund for purchasing islands by one island owner who had granted a conservation easement. That owner had a family foundation, which gave Maine Coast Heritage Trust an unsolicited small grant to launch such a fund with the request it be called the Wild Sea Island Fund. One other foundation added to it, but that was it. The fund sat without further immediate attention from us. Then Earl brought to our attention the extraordinary opportunity to purchase a conservation easement over the end of the Point of Main at the entrance to Machias Bay. This was not an island, but it was a magnificent wild part of the Maine coast.

The property had quite a story to it. In 1968 a developer had proposed an oil unloading terminal for Machias Bay. Rugged Stone Island, just east of the Point of Main, had deep water close to its cliff-like rocky shores and was envisioned as a shoreline that would accommodate the unloading of deeply laden oil tankers. The oil could then be piped under the water to storage and distribution facilities on Point of Main. The developer began enticing landowners with hefty amounts of cash for options to purchase their lands. One home-grown environmentalist held out, and he possessed the key to a feasible project. He was Bruce Sprague, owner of the couple-hundred-acre end of Point of Main. He was a welder and jack-of-all-trades living in an aged farmhouse with no electricity and vehicle access only when the tide was relatively low at a point where a stream flowed through the gravel beach into Machias Bay. He certainly had no money to spare, but he refused to lose his beloved Point of Main to oil interests no matter what the price. He knew and respected Earl Ireland.

Thanks to Earl's relationship with Bruce we were able to get into Bruce's and his wife's kitchen and propose a conservation easement. He was very interested if Maine Coast Heritage Trust would pay him a modest amount for the easement and would arrange and pay for a survey delineating his land from his abutting neighbor, a property line that seemed to be of considerable concern to him. He really did not want to see his homestead on the end of Point of Main be developed in any fashion, and he did not mind giving up the development rights permanently.

For the first time we went to the Maine Coast Heritage Trust board of directors with a proposal to actually pay for a conservation easement. The easement would go to the National Audubon Society, although in later years when Maine Coast Heritage Trust had begun holding real estate interests itself and when National Audubon no longer saw holding conservation easements on such Maine properties as a fit with its mission, it transferred the easement to Maine Coast Heritage Trust. For money we looked to our idle little Wild Sea Island Fund, with which we were doing nothing and for which we had no plans. In those days we had no inkling of the future great capital campaigns of Maine Coast Heritage Trust for the purpose of buying land and conservation easements. The donors to the Wild Sea Island Fund gave us permission to go ahead and spend the money given the extraordinary conservation importance of the Point of Main both scenically and as a way to thwart heavy industrial development in one of Maine's biologically very productive bays. For Maine Coast Heritage Trust the conservation easement at Point of Main was a particularly important land conservation achievement only possible because in Earl we had the right staff person at the right time.

Bruce's intransigence with the oil port developer certainly slowed the plans for an oil port, although the economics of oil port development and the failure of other such proposals to come to fruition indicate that the port probably never would have been built anyway. With the conservation easement on Point of Main and acquisition by The Nature Conservancy of Stone Island, the mouth of Machias Bay is fortunately no longer even a possibility for such a scheme.

❧

My life steadied following marriage to Lisa Heyward, who worked for Maine Coast Heritage Trust one summer very successfully promoting conservation easements, particularly in Frenchman Bay, and later, after our marriage, as staff to the board fundraising committee. I was better able again to give Maine Coast Heritage Trust the attention that it deserved from me and once more take personal satisfaction from my work.

Lisa had first walked in the Maine Coast Heritage Trust door as a graduate student at the Duke School of Forestry who had deep love for and extensive knowledge of Frenchman Bay. In the Maine conservation easement world Lisa deserves credit for having introduced useful new terminology as a result of writing a paper on water access at the request of the State of Maine. The original concerns that led to the creation of Maine Coast Heritage Trust were that the scenic beauty and wild character of coastal islands were being lost to too much and poorly sited development. Ensuring legal public access to islands was not at the time a concern, although a major part of the appeal of boating along the Maine coast is landing on and exploring islands. Many later conservation easements in Maine have provided for legal access by the public, and ensuring public access has become an important goal of most land conservation programs in the state. The early conservation easements, however, did not include provisions allowing use by the public. A landowner granting a conservation easement continued to control access as he or she saw fit—allow it or prohibit it.

At Maine Coast Heritage Trust we realized that one of the benefits of our island conservation easement efforts was that if a conservation easement forbid all building, then as a practical matter people arriving in boats could usually still land and enjoy the experience of a wild Maine island. Without buildings in which to live and with camping by owners rare, there was unlikely to be anyone to be bothered by someone's landing. Fortunately, posting "No Trespassing" signs was not

something that most island owners did. In fact, many island owners—
and our family has felt very much this way with our island—take pleasure from knowing that people enjoy their islands. All that most island
owners want from those landing is respect for the island and avoidance
of abuse. In her paper Lisa recognized that what we then called "forever
wild" conservation easements—those that forbid all development—in
fact did usually mean that islands restricted by such easements were
available for people to land on and enjoy. She labeled this kind of non-
legal access "implicit access." Places where the public has guaranteed
access such as Acadia National Park she identified as having "explicit
access." That was concise and convenient terminology and turned out
to be quite helpful to us when articulating the public benefits of the
Maine Coast Heritage Trust program during the program's early years.

The late 1970s were when Maine Coast Heritage Trust began an
effort that was to develop in later years under subsequent staff to be
a major part of its program: assisting local land trusts. In the 1970s
there were only one or two tiny, low-profile land trust–type organizations in the state, and I knew little or nothing about them. Late in
the decade Margaret Booth of Castine, wife of well-known poet Philip
Booth, was inspired to create a land trust for Castine, the Castine Conservation Trust. I can no longer recall details of our helping her, but I
do remember enjoying getting to know her and Philip and providing
advice. Quite a few years later Castine Conservation Trust recruited
me to do some work for it on a consulting basis, and today it has been
merged into Blue Hill Heritage Trust. With so many local land trusts
having been formed in Maine since Castine led the way, mergers will
no doubt be increasingly common as these small organizations struggle
to remain viable and effective.

In the late 1970s and beginning of the 1980s I found the most intellectual stimulation from the role that Maine Coast Heritage Trust and
I were playing on the national scene. By then what Maine Coast Heritage Trust was accomplishing with the use of the conservation easement

technique had attracted attention from conservationists across America. I occasionally accepted invitations to speak to groups in other states and to participate in conferences on land conservation. Our experiences in Maine were proving useful outside Maine, and interacting with land conservation professionals and volunteers in other states broadened my own knowledge and helped keep me energized.

These were years of much focus on federal income and estate tax law as it applied to conservation easement donations. Congress changed the relevant tax law a couple of times, and the Department of Treasury and the Internal Revenue Service were paying ever closer attention to preventing abuses. Washington's attention to what programs like Maine Coast Heritage Trust were doing led to more and more contact with colleagues in other states and ultimately led to the creation of the Land Trust Exchange, the name of which was later changed to Land Trust Alliance. The lead-up to the creation of the Land Trust Exchange makes an interesting story and one that is important in the history of land conservation by private, nonprofit organizations in the United States.

When in the winter of 1974–75 I was working for the New England Natural Resources Center analyzing the potential onshore impacts of offshore oil development off the New England coast, I became acquainted with the Center's board members including Kingsbury Browne. Kingsbury was a tax attorney with Hill and Barlow in Boston. Shortly after my return to Maine Coast Heritage Trust in 1976, I sought out Kingsbury's advice on some tax matter of concern to Maine Coast Heritage Trust. Kingsbury was absolutely fascinated by tax law as it applied to land conservation. For him spending time on it was almost like a recreation—like golf might be or like sailing always has been to me. Kingsbury told me that he had spent years using the tax law to facilitate the leasing of capital equipment such as jet aircraft and oil tankers. He had realized that the same type of creative thinking that went into making leasing deals as tax advantageous as possible could be applied to land conservation and thereby increase the amount of preserved land in this country. I would ask Kingsbury for advice on a particular matter, and he would reply with a letter and modest bill. Then one day he made a proposal to me that became a turning point in land conservation. "Look," he said, "the advice I am providing you at Maine Coast Heritage Trust would be equally valuable to your sister organizations such as the Society for the Protection of New Hampshire Forests, the Trustees of Reservations in Massachusetts, the Brandywine Conservancy, and other such programs. You could save Maine Coast Heritage Trust money by splitting my bills, and I would get an advantage too. I am in frequent contact with the Department of Treasury and the Internal Revenue Service about land conservation tax issues. My credibility with them would be enhanced by having multiple land conservation organizations as clients. The fees I receive are not important; rather, what is important is being able to say that I represent these organizations."

It was a great idea, and given that Kingsbury could not directly solicit business, he left it to me to contact these other organizations. So began a very modestly priced subscription service of periodic write-ups by Kingsbury on the Hill and Barlow letterhead about federal tax matters of which he thought we should be aware. He also was available to us on the staffs of these organizations to answer specific tax questions that might arise. Thus was created the beginning of a communications network among the organizations sharing the cost of Kingsbury's tax memoranda.

By 1978 calls in Washington for further changes to conservation easement tax law were causing enough concern among us that Kingsbury suggested that he arrange a meeting of executive directors with representatives from Treasury and the Internal Revenue Service. The Brandywine Conservancy agreed to host the gathering at the marvelous old inn in Chadds Ford, Pennsylvania. There we gathered around the big conference table, described our goals and programs and the need for favorable tax treatment of donated conservation easements, and listened to the federal people explain planned changes in the tax law and their concerns about preventing abuse. It was a highly useful and respectful meeting.

After an elegant dinner the first evening I rode up in the elevator with the young attorney representing the Internal Revenue Service. Just to make conversation, I asked if he often was out of Washington attending such meetings. Never before had he been sent to such a meeting, he replied. He explained that conservation easements were a new topic for him, and he was thoroughly enjoying being included in the Chadds Ford meeting.

That attorney was Steve Small. Steve would be assigned to write the IRS regulations on the tax treatment of conservation easements and work closely with us on the drafts. I remember sending him one letter about the degree to which the public derives benefits from the scenic protection of Maine islands, using as an example all the people on what I tend to call the "dude schooners" (perhaps more commonly called "windjammers"), which carry paying passengers on sailing trips of several days along the Maine coast. For these schooner passengers the extraordinary scenery and sense of wildness is one the greatest pleasures of the cruises. Steve would become so intrigued by voluntary land conservation that he would go into private practice representing landowners making major land conservation gifts, write a massive tome on the tax law of conservation easements published by the Land Trust Exchange, write other books for landowners, and join Kingsbury as one of the nation's primary land conservation tax experts.

For Steve the Chadds Ford meeting launched a fine career of making major contributions to American land conservation. Several years later, Steve and I attended a meeting in Montana and flew back across the country together on a beautifully clear day. It was heartwarming to see Steve's enthusiasm as he looked out the window viewing for the first time from the air the vast American landscape, which had come to mean so much to him, pass below the jet's wings.

Kingsbury Browne had arranged the meeting in Chadds Ford to address federal tax issues affecting land conservation, and because of his association with the Lincoln Institute of Land Policy in Cambridge, Massachusetts, he was instrumental in calling together not too long thereafter land conservation professionals to discuss how best to maximize the synergies of cooperating and trading lessons learned in this rapidly expanding field. A staff member of the Lincoln Institute, Allan Spader, handled the details of the meeting and helped facilitate the discussion. The group came to the conclusion that an organization should be formed to advocate for government policies and laws favorable to land conservation, to help land conservation programs network with each other, and to assist in the training of professionals and volunteers. So was conceived the Land Trust Exchange, later to be renamed the Land Trust Alliance.

Four organizations and their executive directors were to be the founders—the Brandywine Conservancy headed by Bill Sellers, the Napa Valley Land Trust under the direction of Joan Vilms, the Iowa Natural Heritage Foundation guided by Mark Ackelson, and Maine Coast Heritage Trust, of which I was executive director. I had huge respect and personal affection for my fellow founders and felt privileged to be part of the foursome. Plans were laid and implemented for the creation of the Land Trust Exchange as a legal nonprofit entity. Allan Spader agreed to leave his research job at the Lincoln Institute to be the executive director. At Boston's well-known environmental hub of 3 Joy Street he found office space. Allan was a very bright visionary, and I give him full credit for creating the vision on which was based the early programs and ultimate success of the Land Trust Exchange.

Maine Coast Heritage Trust's retaining Kingsbury for tax advice, with other organizations then joining Maine Coast Heritage Trust as subscribers to his tax memoranda, had led directly to increased communication between conservation easement programs in various states and then to the birth of the Land Trust Exchange, which as the now Washington, D.C.–based Land Trust Alliance has become a major player on the national land conservation scene. Without Kingsbury and without Maine Coast Heritage Trust, would the course of the networking of land conservation organizations around the country have taken a very different course? Who is to know? For myself I took great satisfaction from working with such stimulating, dedicated colleagues in many parts of the United States.

As the Land Trust Exchange was being established, I was completing six years as executive director of Maine Coast Heritage Trust. With life seemingly stable again, the sea was calling.

8

TRANSITION

The ocean and family adventure beckoned as I wound up my years as executive director of Maine Coast Heritage Trust. On my last day on the job, July 1, 1982, I fear that I scared my successor, recent Yale School of Forestry graduate Davis Hartwell, and angered him too.

Maine Coast Heritage Trust board member Philip Conkling was headed east that morning by helicopter to take a look at forest land he helped manage in far eastern Maine. Maine Coast Heritage Trust was in discussions about a possible project along a Washington County river west of Machias, and Philip's offer of a helicopter ride seemed a great way for Davis to see the potential project area from the air. I would drive down in my old International Harvester four-wheel-drive Scout, take a look with Davis at the land on foot, and drive him home. The helicopter would drop Davis off in a clearing accessible by a logging road that we spotted on a map—a seemingly easy and fun plan. It was a beautiful summer day as I rattled east in the old Scout, and I thought what a special way for Davis to launch his tenure at the Maine Coast Heritage Trust helm. We never thought about the possibility that the helicopter and I might go to different clearings in all that timberland.

I was on time at the rendezvous. I waited and waited. No helicopter and not even any chopper sounds in the distance. In the days before cell phones I had no way to communicate. The only reasonable conclusion seemed to be that the helicopter had encountered some sort of problem and either never taken off or turned back to Bar Harbor airport. I set off on foot alone to take a look at the property of interest and enjoyed a wonderful couple hours of hiking through woods and along the Chandler River. The day's high point was finding the most prolific patch of wild strawberries I have ever seen. They were ripe to perfection. I settled into the grass under the warm July sunshine like a happy bear and plucked one after another from their vines. It was a

gastronomic treat provided by nature in a quiet setting beyond compare. Too bad that Davis was no doubt by then back at the office, having missed a very special way to begin his new job.

Eventually, I tore myself away from my strawberry patch, finished
my explorations, and took off back along the logging roads in the
Scout. There were wet, muddy sections of road, and the Scout was
well splattered when I finally reached the tarred road. I came to the
stop sign at the intersection with Route 1. There, with his thumb out
to passing cars, stood Davis. We both were dumbfounded when we
recognized each other. "Where on earth have you been?" was the common question. Davis seemed quite irritated when he climbed in. To
my horror I discovered that he seemed to suspect that I had purposely
planned his being dropped into the Maine woods to be tested on his
ability to find his way out and home all by himself, perhaps some sort
of sophomoric hazing on my part. It was several minutes before I was
sure that I had him convinced otherwise. So ended my Maine Coast
Heritage Trust executive directorship—satiated with wild strawberries
in a mud-splattered Scout with my successor wondering what he had
gotten himself into.

With Maine Coast Heritage Trust duties handed over, I turned
my attention to final voyage preparations. The prior winter we had
bought a Bowman 46 yawl, wanting a strongly built and forgiving boat
for venturing farther afield as a family. I had found the boat for sale
in an icy slip at Boston's Constitution Marina the previous January.
British-designed and -built, she was extremely strong in her hull and
rig. Because of the rugged weather and sea conditions around the British Isles, British boats tend to be particularly robust, and this fiberglass
Bowman 46 was very much so at the same time as having exceptionally
lovely lines, the flow of which made for happy times just looking at
her. She had been built only six years earlier for a young couple who
had planned to take her around the world and was consequently very
well equipped. Reportedly, their cruise ended prematurely when having arrived from England at Annapolis, the wife decided enough was
enough. That does happen. Then a Boston banker had owned her.

Her condition was a surprising way from pristine given that she was not very old, but problems were primarily cosmetic and could be dealt with. Some Bowman 46s had deep keels, and some like ours were built with centerboards in somewhat shallower keels. For our family plans of coastal and offshore voyaging the boat was a treasure, although some years later her relatively small British rig would prove frustrating in the frequently light summer winds of Maine and induce me to sell her.

We named the Bowman *Meridian* for high noon in our lives. How we viewed that point in our lives and the impetus for preparing to pack family aboard a sailboat and head off was enshrined in a wonderful quotation from Richard John MacCullagh's book *Vikings Wake*. We framed and mounted the quotation in the cabin on *Meridian's* main bulkhead:

What if the spell of a place falls upon a youthful heart, and the bright horizons call! Many a thing will keep till the world's work is done, and youth is only a memory. When the Old Enchanter came to my door, laden with dreams, I reached out with both hands. For I knew that he would not be lured with the gold that I might later offer, when age had come upon me.

I hugely appreciated Lisa's supporting my heeding the call of the bright horizons. With Kristin at age ten, Thor age six, and Chafee age four we assembled clothing, equipment, and school supplies and prepared for our Labor Day departure from Brooklin.

Originally, my hope was to have Alaska as our destination, but reality set in and caused us to limit our plans to a cruise to the West Indies and back. The following June when we creamed up Frenchman Bay in driving, cold rain for our homecoming, the flags of the nations whose tropic isles we had visited snapped at our starboard spreader. There flew the flags of Great Britain, France, Holland, Antigua, St. Kitts/Nevis, and the Bahamas. We had had adventures underway, on shore, and in the water, and the children had been home-schooled with correspondence courses from Baltimore's Calvert School—an adventure in itself for parent and child. What fascinated me very much on our return to Maine waters was to hear Kristin, Thor, and Chafee exclaim about the beauty of the Maine islands. In years past they never had indicated any

special appreciation of Maine's magnificent coast. The months of cruising other shores and waters had given them new perspective on their
home area.

For me the cruise had given me my own new perspective on Maine,
a deepened recognition of how much I was tied to its landscape and
people. I had loved the sailing, the navigating, seeing so much of the
East Coast and the West Indies and Bahamas; the snorkeling, the new-
to-us sport of windsurfing, and the concentrated time with the family.
On the other hand, I had missed Maine more than I had anticipated.
In the fall before heading offshore from Charleston, South Carolina, on
a direct course to St. Thomas, I had flown to New York for a meeting.
Already I had been away from Maine for two months, and as I sat on
the airplane, part of me wished that I was headed home to Maine from
New York rather than back to the boat waiting in Charleston.

En route north in the spring we stopped at Norfolk, Virginia, and there
I received an unexpected telephone call that was to take me back into
conservation work. Hank Foster had already twice steered me to opportunities: first with his suggestion about encouraging yacht clubs to
become more active in coastal conservation efforts, the suggestion that
led to the conservation cruise in the first *Eggemoggin* under the American Littoral Society flag; and then secondly, when as board chair of the
New England Natural Resources Center he encouraged me to undertake the analysis of how well equipped the New England states were to
cope with the onshore impacts of offshore oil development.

Hank was on the phone. By that day in May 1983 he had taken
over as president of the W. Alton Jones Foundation, which had become
a funder of the Land Trust Exchange, still barely fledged as an organization. Allan Spader as executive director was trying to get it launched
properly out of the office at 3 Joy Street in Boston, the home of the
Appalachian Mountain Club, which also housed other environmental
organizations. Hank wanted to know whether I would be willing to
act as a consultant and help guide Allan, who was new to managing a

nonprofit. The W. Alton Jones Foundation would provide a grant to pay me. Hank believed that my experience from my years as Maine Coast Heritage Trust's executive director would help Allan. We agreed to chat more when *Meridian* arrived home.

In July I went to Boston to explore with Allan how I might assist the Land Trust Exchange. There was the potential for the issue to be touchy, for Allan was the executive director and I was being sent by a funder to provide guidance. I wondered how Allan would be feeling about the proposed arrangement, but he greeted me warmly. He took me to lunch and invited along a young woman who had very recently started work as office manager following her graduation from college. Until that day I had not heard of Caroline Pryor, who dreamed of a career in marine sciences but, needing a job, had wandered into 3 Joy Street, seen on the bulletin board a notice that the Land Trust Exchange sought some help upstairs, and begun tackling basic office tasks for Allan. Little could any of us know as we sat at lunch in Boston how soon Caroline's and my lives would become closely intertwined in a working and friendship relationship, our friendship continuing to this day. We sketched out a role for me, and I flew home to Maine.

Within a very short number of weeks that summer Allan began alerting me by telephone to impending financial collapse at the Land Trust Exchange. Revenues were not going to cover overhead, and the organization was rapidly running out of cash to pay salaries, rent, and telephone service. This very new nonprofit with such a promising vision was bankrupt. The executive committee and I had to terminate the staff, make plans to close the office, and notify funders. There seemed no immediate future for the concept of a trade association-type of entity to serve the growing land trust community.

No sooner had the word been passed to funders than Hank Foster was on the telephone again. The vision for the Land Trust Exchange was too good to let go, said Hank. The W. Alton Jones Foundation was willing to continue providing financial support. Would I, he asked, be willing to become executive director? I had only been back in Maine a couple of months since our return from the Caribbean in *Meridian*, and my future plans were still in flux. I remember my answer to Hank clearly. "I am not moving to Boston," I said, "but if the Land Trust Exchange comes to Maine, I will try to resurrect it." Two other foundations, the William and Flora Hewlett Foundation and the David and Lucile Packard Foundation, were willing to continue support too. With a smaller budget there was reason to hope that we could be successful. The board of directors did not hesitate to agree.

We had already rehired Caroline to help close down the Boston office, having realized that we needed someone who knew the situation there, and those of us who had met her were impressed by her competence. She made herself famous by calling one day to say that the Exchange owned hundreds of dollars' worth of postage stamps. "Sell them!" was my emphatic response, and so she did, peddling them to the other nonprofits in the 3 Joy Street building. She clearly was resourceful in getting things done; we needed someone who knew something about day-to-day operations; and I would need help in Maine when we completed the office move. The light bulb went on. On one of my many telephone calls with her about details of closing down in Boston I asked, "Would you have any interest in coming to Maine?" Except for a brief visit with her family as a child, she had never set foot in the state. It was September with the long, cold winter stretching ahead. She was a young woman who would be moving to a very quiet winter social scene on Mount Desert Island. Worryingly, the financial stability of the Land Trust Exchange was far from assured. "Caroline," I said, having conferred with the executive committee, "we will make two promises to you. We will feed you and keep you warm until spring." She came.

9

WITH A NATIONAL MEGAPHONE— THE LAND TRUST EXCHANGE

Caroline Pryor's decision to cast her lot with the nearly bankrupt Land Trust Exchange and move to Maine, where she had never been, and work with me, whom she barely knew, showed courage, self-reliance, and self-confidence. Those traits were to prove invaluable as she settled into a new life and made herself a critical part of resurrecting this organization which had failed in its first attempt to get off the ground. Command central was to be my attic, somewhat insulated against the oncoming Maine winter, with just enough heat to get by, and accessed by a wooden ladder from my kitchen. It was a spartan office, for sure, but very Maine in its frugality.

Word-processing computers remained in their infancy. I already was invested in a portable Kaypro with the CP/M operating system and was used to it. Why not get one for Caroline too, I thought. We sent a letter off to Kaypro describing our worthy endeavors and asking whether they might donate one of their machines. At no charge back came an even better one than I already had. Both of us were now equipped with word processors, and, without desks, we sat side by side at a door laid across file cabinets. With a great view out the dormer window looking into Pretty Marsh Harbor, Caroline and I went to work to rebuild the Land Trust Exchange.

We saw our mission as twofold. The first part was to develop and maintain an effective communications network linking land trusts all around the United States so that they could learn from each other and avoid needlessly reinventing the wheel. The name Land Trust Exchange put the emphasis on that aspect of the work—exchanging lessons learned. The second part of our mission was to use the collective voice of the land trusts to affect federal government policies, especially tax policies, that directly impacted land conservation. The name of the organization was changed to Land Trust Alliance after my time of being involved, the word Alliance seemingly putting the emphasis on trying to affect public policies. I had experience in both arenas, but having been in the leadership of one of the most successful conservation easement programs in the nation at a time when that land conservation technique was still relatively new and evolving, I probably had the most to offer personally in trying to help land trusts exchange information.

We had an exceptionally able and dedicated group of board members, advisors, and supporting foundation staff members to back us up. The other original three co-founders with me remained on the board— Bill Sellers of Brandywine Conservancy, Mark Ackelson of Iowa Natural Heritage Foundation, and Joan Vilms of Napa Valley Land Trust. Kingsbury Browne, whose epistles on federal tax matters had demonstrated the advantages of land trusts' sharing information and whose leadership on communicating with the Department of Treasury and the Internal Revenue Service had taught us the policy benefits of collective action, remained deeply engaged as our godfather. Another somewhat fatherly figure senior in age to many of us was kindly and hugely committed Bob Augsburger, who chaired the board of the Land Trust Exchange and served as Executive Director of Peninsula Open Space Trust in the San Francisco Bay area.

Other accomplished land trust professionals had been recruited to serve on the board too, people like Brian Steen of Big Sur Land Trust, Tom Schmidt of Western Pennsylvania Conservancy, Hans Neuhauser of the Georgia Conservancy, and the veteran Gordon Abbott of the Trustees of Reservations in Massachusetts. Gordon shared my passion for sailing and cruising and was a fellow member of the Cruising Club of America. He loved to chat. To the tolerant amusement, hopefully not irritation, of our colleagues, he and I not infrequently launched into lengthy side conversations about sailboats, almost forgetting in our enthusiasm for sailing that we were together to work on land conservation. Another stalwart who joined the board relatively early was Jean Hocker of the Jackson Hole Land Trust. As it turned out, she would succeed me a few years later as Land Trust Exchange executive director. This was a group of people who shared a deep commitment to conserving the nation's natural land resources and who very much enjoyed each other's company as we strived together toward common goals. Bob Augsburger's son once accompanied his father to an Exchange event and, as reported by Bob, said, "Dad, this is the nicest group of people with whom you have ever worked."

Our board of directors, representing a diverse array of land trusts from many parts of the country, gave us a respectable beginning for developing a broad membership base of land trusts. Our foundation friends would keep us going for the time being, but operating revenues were going to have to be found elsewhere relatively soon. Just as small businesses are encouraged to join trade associations and chambers of commerce, land trusts were encouraged to join the Land Trust Exchange. Membership dues were seen as a crucial part of our revenue stream. What we could offer land trusts was access to information and education that would help them be more effective and accelerate the pace of their land conservation successes.

A key component of our educational efforts was the organization's fledgling journal *Exchange*. Caroline acted as editor with backup from me. We put our heads together on ideas for articles, and she recruited authors, rode herd on deadlines, edited submissions, selected photographs, and worked with a graphics firm on final layout. It was a big undertaking for our tiny office. She learned on the job, bringing her many innate talents to bear. The end products were very good and proved useful to land trust staffs and boards. The journal played a key role in the revitalization of the Land Trust Exchange and in underscoring its value as a communication and information hub.

We also saw the need for a national conference of land trusts. Speakers could address major issues confronting land trusts; workshops could provide training on a wide variety of topics; and land trust personnel could get to know colleagues from across the country, not only enjoyable and educational but helpful when collaborating on public policy matters. A conference would take a huge amount of organizational work, but hosting one seemed a vital step for the Land Trust Exchange. Caroline deserves much credit for her very clever idea of calling it a Rally. The name generated quick excitement and played an important role in making the first Rally, held at the Smithsonian in Washington, D.C., a huge success. As I recall, attendance was at least 300 people, and our keynote speaker, Senator John Chafee of Rhode Island, enhanced the gathering's stature.

National Rallies continue on a regularly scheduled basis to this day with much higher attendance figures, the concept's having proven exceptionally worthwhile at the outset and continuing to be so. Land trust staff and board members have frequently commented over the years how these events recharge their batteries, sending them home with renewed enthusiasm for their land conservation work. This positive mental effect of the Rallies is probably as important as any other aspects of the events.

Our publishing efforts soon extended beyond the journal. Tax attorney Steve Small, whom I first met at the meeting which Kingsbury Browne had arranged at Brandywine Conservancy with representatives of Treasury and the Internal Revenue Service in the late 1970s, had moved on to the private sector. Steve's attendance at the Brandywine meeting and his subsequent assignment to write the new federal tax regulations governing conservation easement donations had left him fascinated with the land conservation world and the conservation easement technique in particular. After leaving government service he wrote a definitive work on federal tax law regarding conservation easements, the massive *Federal Tax Law of Conservation Easements*. He asked the Land Trust Exchange to undertake publishing the first edition, which we did. We also worked with the talented Elizabeth Watson at the National Trust for Historic Preservation on co-publishing a booklet for professional real estate appraisers giving guidance on appraising both conservation easements on land and preservation easements on buildings.

Congress seemed to be growing increasingly concerned by reports of abuses of conservation easements. New tax laws and the regulations which Steve Small had written while still with the Internal Revenue Service were attempts to curtail deductions from federal income and estate taxes for easements that were not properly voluntary gifts and which did not meet standards of public benefit. Nonetheless, clever and greedy people sometimes continued to find ways to obtain profitable deductions that should not have been taken. We recognized that non-profit land trusts were being created to reward developers and others for projects that had little or no conservation merit. Gordon Abbott called these entities "fly-by-night land trusts," and their worrisome existence caused us to focus on how to create a mechanism for self-policing of land trusts. We much preferred self-policing to the heavy hand of control by new laws that Congress might pass. Our early discussions led ultimately, after my time of involvement, to the Land Trust Alliance's developing clearly articulated Standards and Practices for land trusts and then a system of accreditation. This effort to prevent abuse of the tax code and to ensure that land conservation is conducted in the public interest has stretched over many years and continues.

We quickly saw the need to educate Congress about all the good that was being accomplished with conservation easements. We needed to convince House and Senate not to throw out the baby with the bath water as they sought to rein in abuse of the easement technique. That led to yet another publishing project for the Land Trust Exchange. We published a quite handsome special issue of the journal *Exchange* illustrated with wonderful photographs of lands protected by conservation easements and good articles describing what was being accomplished in many parts of the nation and by whom. This we widely distributed.

Eerily reminiscent of how my start as executive director of Maine Coast Heritage Trust had been seriously marred in the early months by family tragedy, I was hit again by trauma in my family, this time marriage breakup, not many months after moving the Land Trust Exchange to my attic and becoming executive director. In both cases hardworking, very bright, dedicated young women colleagues kept the organizations forging ahead even as I was distracted by child responsibilities and getting on with my life. I had relied on Janet Milne at Maine Coast Heritage Trust; I relied on Caroline Pryor at the Land Trust Exchange. Both organizations and my own reputation for carrying through on professional commitments were fortunate that Janet and Caroline so capably assumed additional workloads.

I seriously wondered whether because of my children I could travel as much as leading a national organization would require. Bob Barrett of the staff of the William and Flora Hewlett Foundation was a vital supporter of the Exchange. I told Bob that I did not see how I could be away from home as much as I thought would be a necessary part of the job. I will never forget Bob's reply. "Ben," he said, "we don't care if you travel or not. If you need someone to travel for the Exchange and you cannot do it, tell us, and we will give you the funds to hire someone." Wow, what reassuring support! As it turned out, I did not travel a great deal but was able to do what was really necessary and could call on Caroline too. The Hewlett Foundation was hugely helpful to us, but we did not need funds to hire yet another person to be on the road.

It was time for the Land Trust Exchange to vacate the attic. The Exchange required more space anyway, for Caroline and I had reached the point of needing administrative assistance. Marie Stivers brought ability and good humor to our new office in downtown Bar Harbor, and the three of us made a cohesive and fun team that lasted for the duration of the Exchange's having its office on Mount Desert Island.

Once I got my feet back under me, I think I did a good job for the Land Trust Exchange, but my heart was never into the day-to-day work of the Exchange in the way that it had been into Maine Coast Heritage Trust. Running what was essentially a trade association was less person-ally satisfying than working to preserve special places in Maine. When Maine Coast Heritage Trust had succeeded in helping a landowner per-manently protect the natural qualities of a beautiful coastal island, that success truly made me exuberant. The lead-up to such successes was also rewarding on a daily basis—identifying worthy properties, gaining access to the owners, pitching the case for preservation, working on the details, and finally getting papers signed.

Basically, I loved doing land deals. I remember one day when I was representing The Conservation Fund in Maine after my Land Trust Exchange years. The Fund's president, Pat Noonan, walked me to the elevator as I was departing after a visit to the head office in Arlington,

Virginia. Pat had done a great job lining up experienced land conservation people all over the country to help The Conservation Fund pursue its land conservation agenda. I laughed heartily when Pat commented that the Fund was full of people who had discovered that they really did not want to run organizations but rather preferred to spend their time doing land deals. I certainly fit his mold.

I knew that I would not be executive director of the Land Trust Exchange for the long run. Not only was I going to get restive, but as the Exchange became more secure financially, Bar Harbor, Maine, would not be the ideal headquarters for an organization serving the entire country and working on policy issues in the nation's capital. It became increasingly evident that the Exchange eventually should base in Washington. When the time arrived that the Exchange really needed to move in order to continue to develop its potential, I clearly would be leaving. My roots in Maine were far too deep by then to consider moving myself.

I had assumed the executive directorship in the early fall of 1983. By three years later I was married to Dianna, a clinical mental health counselor on Mount Desert Island introduced to me by our mutual sailing friends Tina and Bob Hinckley. Dianna joined my life along with her school-age daughters, Melissa and Bethany.

I was thinking of an extended sailing cruise again, convinced that the Exchange was ready for the move to Washington. The search for a successor was fun and an opportunity to meet some fine candidates. The pleasing selection by the board of our own Jean Hocker would prove astute. By the time of the second National Rally, this one at Asilomar in California in 1987, the changes had been announced.

I loved my farewell from the land trust community. Several hundred people were at the final dinner of the Rally, assembled in the large dining hall of Asilomar. I and others made appropriate comments from the stage, and then I was handed a going-away present to a roomful of warm laughter. I am known for a loud voice and usually not needing a microphone for speeches. It may be genetic, for my father used to say that my mother did not need her telephone to communicate long distance. I yell on the telephone too. My gift from the Land Trust

Exchange, presented with fanfare on the Asilomar stage, was a megaphone.

Caroline wanted to go to Washington no more than I did, her own roots in Maine growing rapidly, but she did assist Jean Hocker with the transition. Jean succeeded in taking the organization to a whole new level before she too yielded the reins years later. In Washington, soon under its new name of Land Trust Alliance, it became ever more effective in working on national policy issues affecting land conservation and in offering training to land trusts nationwide. A huge amount of effort with many people involved went into improving the accountability and self-policing of land trusts through developing both the Standards and Practices and the accreditation program.

In the case of both Maine Coast Heritage Trust and the Land Trust Exchange, I left as executive director when the organizations were financially stable, had a fine track record, and enjoyed a high degree of respect, but they were still tiny in terms of staff and budget. Both organizations went on to grow exponentially under subsequent executive directors with staff, budget, and programs of a scale that I and the board members in my time could hardly have conceived. Under more skilled builders of effective bureaucracies than I ever could have been, both organizations have done great work and continue to do so.

10

ACADIA NATIONAL PARK

Ken Burns subtitled his widely seen Public Broadcasting film on our national parks *America's Best Idea*. His inspiration for that subtitle came from historian, novelist, and environmentalist Wallace Stegner's having called the national parks "the best idea we ever had." My over forty years of living close to a national park has been a privilege that few Americans experience. Acadia National Park has been a huge part of my life over all those years—all three districts of it on Mount Desert Island, Schoodic Point, and Isle au Haut. It has been and remains a place of fun recreation, rejuvenation, and healthy exercise, of nature observation and education, of intellectual stimulation and inspiration, of policy involvement, and of lasting friendships formed. Schoodic and Isle au Haut have been treasured sailing destinations. We have anchored off both many, many times.

Acadia's roots with sailors go deep. In fact, a summer sailing cruise lay at the very genesis of Acadia National Park. In 1871 Charles W. Eliot, president of Harvard College, sailed from Boston to Mount Desert Island in a small sloop and was there joined by family members including his son Charles. Inspired by this experience the younger Eliot returned many times to study the island's natural history and with colleagues began calling for protection of the island's natural qualities for the benefit of the public. After the younger Eliot's death his father sought to carry out his son's vision and cooperated with George Dorr in the formation of the Hancock County Trustees of Public Reservations, which acquired the first properties that ultimately were to become part of Acadia National Park.

Were I to choose one most overwhelmingly magical time in Acadia National Park, it might be a cold, silent winter night in 1997 when Acadia was buried in deep snow. On our cross-country skis Dianna and I skied around the Witch Hole Pond carriage road loop. From one side of the cloudless sky a full moon brightly illuminated our path. Opposite in the heavens glowed the Hale-Bopp comet. We saw not another soul the whole time in that great cathedral of Nature.

Some winters snowy owls come from their summer nesting grounds on the tundra of the high Arctic to the open granite summits of Acadia's mountains. We hoped that perhaps we could catch the thrill of seeing one of these extraordinary birds. On a relatively warm early December day when ice on the rocks underfoot was not of concern, we biked to a trailhead, then climbed Sargent Mountain to be rewarded not only by spotting a snowy owl but by seeing it swoop close by us in flight, its great white wings of startlingly wide span.

The Witch Hole Pond area of the Park, near our Salisbury Cove home, has been a focal point for exercise—skiing, ice skating, walks, and biking—and for seeing wildlife. Otters, beavers, wood ducks, buffleheads, black ducks, mallards, turtles, owls, coyotes, flocks of migrating songbirds, even an albino deer have enhanced the pleasure of innumerable trips into Acadia there. Elsewhere in Acadia we have enjoyed all that too and climbed to most of the summits, soaking in the spectacular views over hills, woods, ocean, bays, and islands.

Some people seem immune to appreciating the restorative magic of Acadia's scenery and wildlife. When in 1976 I was working at the Center for Research and Advanced Study at the University of Maine in Portland, I was pleased to bring my boss to Mount Desert Island for his first-ever visit. He had been an engineer with Bell Labs. As we approached the island on Route 3 in Trenton, he was describing some of his past engineering endeavors. Coming around a curve, I tried to stop him in mid-sentence to proudly point out his first view of the hills of Mount Desert. He barely paused or looked and was without comment.

Even beloved friends have shown inability to "get it." Dianna and I were hiking around Witch Hole Pond with another couple with whom we are very close. Quite a ways behind us were other walkers. Suddenly otters appeared from under the water close to our path, and three of the four of us stopped in fascination. "Hurry up, hurry up!" our friend tried to command his wife, Dianna, and me, continuing, "We'll have to follow those people coming up behind us!"

"I want to watch the otters," replied his wife.

"Oh, forget the otters!" Ever since that rejoinder Dianna and I have used the word "otters" as code for not wanting people behind on a trail to catch up with us.

My introduction to close association with Acadia was twofold at the outset of my conservation career and moving to Maine year-round. Because Acadia National Park was the first agency in Maine to begin acquiring conservation easements, I was involved with the Park from my first day on the job at Maine Coast Heritage Trust in 1971. Moving to Pretty Marsh the following spring I immediately began hiking and skiing in the Park and swimming and ice skating at the ponds bordered by the Park lands. My highly energized golden retriever Salty loved Acadia as much as I in those days before the eventually needed crackdown on unleashed dogs. Having so much public and beautiful land near our house on Mount Desert Island was one of the finest parts of settling on the island.

Discussed earlier are the Acadia conservation easement program and my years of involvement with Acadia's trying to gain public support for a Master Plan, which eventually passed Congress in 1986. My working for Maine Coast Heritage Trust is why I so quickly developed close relationships with senior Park staff and learned about management issues facing the Park.

Outside the Superintendent's office door at Acadia National Park headquarters hangs a varnished board with little brass plates listing all the superintendents throughout the Park's history. Looking at that board one day I suddenly felt more of an old-timer than I wanted to feel when I realized that I have known more than half of the men whose names are on that board. Some did a better job than others, as with any organization, but recent superintendents have been outstanding. Two, Sheridan Steele and his immediate predecessor, Paul Haertel, are close personal friends. Paul, in fact, has been an invaluable crew member for me on sailing trips to and in the Caribbean. Others on the Park staff over the years have been friends too. The privilege of being acquainted with many bright, dedicated, skilled employees of the National Park Service has given me great appreciation of and respect for those who work for government conservation agencies. This is the same enthusiastic reaction I had during my years representing The Conservation Fund in Maine and partnering with men and women working for the U.S. Fish and Wildlife Service, the sister agency of the National Park Service within the U.S. Department of the Interior.

In the mid-1990s Governor Angus King appointed me to the Acadia National Park Advisory Commission. The Commission had been established by Congress in the Master Plan legislation to assure local residents that they would have a forum to voice their perspectives about Park matters. Had the Park not experienced so much anti-federal sentiment during the years of trying to get a Master Plan approved, the Commission would never have been created. The early members of the Commission, some appointed by surrounding towns, some by the Secretary of the Interior, and some by Maine's Governor, tended to harbor considerable reservations about the national park, and the Park managers found the Commission's existence a mixed blessing.

A decade later aging and retirements took their toll on the original composition of the Commission; hard feelings of the Master Plan years seemed to soften; and new commissioners were appointed to replace those departing. A surprisingly rapid shift occurred from a preponderance of people less than enthusiastic about much of what Acadia stands for to a group eager to help and support the Park. I was part of that crop of new commissioners friendly to the Park and its needs.

The Commission has no veto authority, the word "advisory" in its name clearly underscoring that. The governing legislation mandates, though, that the Secretary of the Interior (in practice, primarily meaning the Acadia superintendent) "shall consult with the Commission on matters relating to the management and development of the Park." Included in this broad charge is advising on acquisitions of land and conservation easements.

To the merriment of my fellow commissioners I was unwittingly silenced by my very own daughter, Chafee, on one of the first matters of substance debated during my early years on the Commission. Acadia had gift shops at the Jordan Pond House, Thunder Hole, and on the summit of Cadillac Mountain. Under consideration was whether some or all should be closed or reduced in square footage and whether the inventory should be limited and touristy non-essentials like T-shirts and plastic lobsters eliminated. I strongly questioned the need for any sort of shop at the summit of Cadillac. There were plenty of places elsewhere on Mount Desert Island for tourists to shop to their hearts' content. There were no gift shops on the summits of Acadia's other mountains, reachable only on foot. Why reward those scaling Cadillac in an automobile or bus with shopping at the top?

Park officials wanted the Commission members to visit the Cadillac Mountain gift shop. Up we went in vans on one of those extremely hot, hazy days that Maine fortunately experiences very rarely. Standing with the other commissioners chatting outside the gift shop I suddenly heard, "Dad!" Spinning around I found Chafee with sweat pouring off her, red in the face, and panting. With her were several women friends of hers and mine. With inadequate water and no money they had just hiked up Cadillac. Out came my wallet and credit card as I treated all of those hot, thirsty women to bottles of water from the gift shop. I objected to the gift shop no more, but I was glad that the Park did place limits on types of items to sell and at the Jordan Pond House converted some of the gift shop space to an area for interpretive exhibits.

I have no doubt served more than enough years on the Acadia Advisory Commission—sixteen years according to the newspaper at the end of what turned out to be my first stint. I was sorry to be replaced, though, and, in fact, the Park Service had recommended my reappointment. No way, however, was Paul LePage, by then Governor of Maine, going to reappoint me, probably because I am a registered Democrat, even though the Acadia Advisory Commission should be completely non-partisan. He sent me out to pasture.

Five years later, in 2016, I was back on thanks to a Secretary of the Interior appointment. I returned just as Acadia National Park faced an array of very important issues demanding Commission attention—expansion of the Park at Schoodic's requiring Congressional legislation to clarify the legality of the new acquisition, uncertainty about whether harvesters of clams and marine worms may legally harvest between high and low tide in Acadia, and transportation planning for this era's massive overcrowding in high season.

The other great concern of the Commission is funding for the Park. Congress has failed to provide sufficient money for years, leaving Acadia with many unfilled, important staff positions and other problems. Making matters worse, perhaps much so, the presidential election of 2016 ushered in a political atmosphere in Washington dangerously hostile to proper functioning of the entire National Park System.

Even as I was enjoying the official connection with Acadia during my early years on the Commission, Dianna was deeply engaged with Acadia too, serving on the board of Friends of Acadia, for six busy years as chairperson. Most of those were years when Ken Olson ably led the staff as president of Friends of Acadia and, working closely with Dianna and other board members, made Friends of Acadia one of the most respected Friends groups in the nation. I watched from the sidelines but admired and appreciated the many ways that Friends of Acadia was using advocacy and private philanthropy to help Park managers operate and preserve our outstanding national park.

Dianna introduced me to her favorite activity in Acadia at the time—horseback riding on the carriage roads. When we started dating, she lived next to the Park with sixteen horses. Except for a couple of weeks on a Montana dude ranch as a child, I had no experience with horses, and I am not sure why I did not quickly run the other way. That first summer I learned a lot about shoveling. More than one person assumed that I was just a new barn hand as I pushed wheelbarrows full of manure. The reason for all the horses was her ring riding school and guided trail rides. Probably to the detriment of the doctoral dissertation she was writing at the time, she broke away frequently that summer to ride on the carriage roads with me. I absolutely loved the rides in Acadia.

As I became more comfortable in the saddle, we frequently would kick the horses into thrilling gallops—until one afternoon with Dianna's horse's tail streaming just ahead of my horse's nose I watched in horror as a foreleg of her horse broke through the gravel surface and Dianna flew over his neck and onto her head in the carriage road. Fortunately, she was wearing a helmet, and the horse got to his feet uninjured. Dianna was seriously concussed, though, her pupils large and her conversation making little sense as I helped her back into the saddle and slowly led her horse back to the barn. That hole in the carriage road which could have killed Dianna and her horse was indicative of carriage roads very much in need of repair. The problem was well recognized, and not too long thereafter private philanthropists, many in response to active and effective solicitation by Friends of Acadia, provided funds so that the National Park Service could rebuild these roads so emblematic of this national park.

By the following year we married and moved to where trail riding in Acadia would have required trailering Dianna's two remaining horses. Sadly, we rode in the Park no more. As the years went by, we missed the riding less and less as ever more bikes appeared on the carriage roads, increasing the chances of dangerous spooking of horses. We bought bikes ourselves and have enjoyed years of that kind of riding in Acadia.

Our summer location on Eggemoggin Reach and owning a cruising sailboat puts the Isle au Haut District of Acadia within an easy sail. The low cone of Isle au Haut's Champlain Mountain is visible from many vantage points close to Center Harbor, made blue by the distance on sunny days as it rises above the dark green of much closer islands. The low slopes of that gentle mountain always beckon to me when they are within view, and they were the focus of my attention one afternoon, probably in my late teens, when I sat on an island sandbar gazing at Isle au Haut as I tried to make decisions about my life's direction.

It is usually a lovely sail to Isle au Haut, either through the Merchant

Row archipelago of seemingly countless ledges and picture-postcard spruce and fir-covered islands or, occasionally, past Marshall Island to port and around the drama of Isle au Haut's rugged outer shore facing the open ocean. About half of Isle au Haut is in the national park. Two beautiful anchorages on the western side of the island provide direct access to the Park—Duck Harbor, a long, narrow cove, and much larger Moore Harbor. Neither is an ideal all-weather anchorage, but both are comfortable most of the time in summer conditions.

Two or three times a summer we head for Isle au Haut for a night or two and as much hiking as we can fit into the available time. The trails of Isle au Haut are similar to those on Mount Desert, but with far fewer visitors to this district of the Park, the trails feel wilder and more remote. Occasionally, we walk up the dirt road from where we have landed to the small fishing village and general store near the island's north end. It has its own anchorage with a town dock in the Isle au Haut Thorofare, the narrow passage inside big Kimball Island.

We usually visit the eastern end of the Acadia archipelago under sail two or three times a summer as well—anchored in Winter Harbor or farther out off the Acadia National Park float at Frazer Point in the Schoodic District. From the Frazer Point anchorage the rowing and stand-up paddleboarding up the outlet of Mill Creek north of the anchorage are superb—a narrow, protected waterway, serenely beautiful and often alive with birds. Here we once witnessed the drama of a furious osprey driving a marauding bald eagle away from its nest high in a spruce. Schoodic also has become a frequent destination by car since Dianna joined the board of Schoodic Institute at Acadia National Park (the full if lengthy name) and collared me into joining its Advisory Council.

The development of Schoodic Institute has been a major happening for Acadia. My own interest in it was captured by the expansive vision for it developed by Dr. Mike Soukup. Mike was recruited out of retirement following serving as chief scientist of the National Park Service to be Schoodic Institute's president and CEO for three years. When Mike was still with the National Park Service, he had worked with Congress creating research and education centers at nearly twenty national parks. At Schoodic he had the opportunity to actually run one of his creations—and the one with the most magnificent facilities in the National Park System, the rehabilitated former naval station within the Schoodic District of Acadia that is now the Schoodic Education and Research Center campus. There the Institute manages the residential campus and operates education and research programs with a host of partners. The Institute facilitates research on environmental changes important to Acadia's natural resource managers seeking to increase Acadia's resilience in the face of a warming climate, trains teachers and others, explores the intersection of art and science, and develops best practices and protocols for citizen science as well as providing citizen science opportunities to people from middle school students to adults of all ages. Its national and, indeed, international potential was encapsulated in Mike Soukup's own words:

Schoodic Institute at Acadia National Park expands the traditional role of a national park as a vacation destination into a regional and community catalyst for ecosystem research, conservation training, and education. It uses its bold physical and inspirational location as a place of personal and professional transformation.

Mike roped me into one of his signature efforts at Schoodic Institute, what he called "the Short Course." This was the reinstitution of a course that the National Park Service for some years had run for managers of parks and reserves, including marine reserves, in other nations. Mike asked if I would speak briefly to a group of such managers from Chile and Colombia on the topic of how Acadia National Park had worked with private landowners to preserve with conservation easements land scenically and ecologically important to the Park. Honored to be asked, I went to extra effort to prepare a good talk. Only after I had prepared it did it dawn on me to ask whether my audience understood English. "Oh, no," was Mike's unnerving reply.

In this globalized day and age many people are used to giving talks that must be translated, but I had never done it. Much simplified and shortened to give time for translating every word, it seemed to go over well, though, with great energy in the room and excellent questions, all translated. I came away energized myself and awakened

to the international significance of the National Park Service's helping train managers of major parks on other continents. Interestingly,
the participants from Colombia and Chile made clear their surprise
at the extent to which landowner altruism and private philanthropy
have played such major roles in land conservation in the United States.
These attributes apparently are less present in the Latin culture.

Mike's successor, Mark Berry, I had known when as executive
director of Downeast Lakes Land Trust he was an applicant for funds
from the Land for Maine's Future Program while I was on the Land
for Maine's Future Board, service which I will discuss in a following
chapter. He had made a good impression on me. In 2011 he had presented the highest-scoring Land for Maine's Future project. Downeast
Lakes Land Trust had established an enviable record in innovative forestland conservation including being one of the first land trusts in the
nation to raise money by selling carbon credits on the California Carbon Exchange—no mean feat for a tiny nonprofit from remote Grand
Lake Stream, Maine. Soon after Mike Soukup had announced that he
planned to retire, I saw Mark at Schoodic when he was speaking at a
conference on the topic of his selling the carbon credits. When I spotted him alone at the dirty-dish counter in the cafeteria following lunch,
I jumped from my seat, told him that Mike was leaving, and asked him
if he might be interested. Dianna followed up with Mark; the typical
national search ensued; and, lo and behold, Grand Lake Stream was
soon the loser and Schoodic the gainer.

Research ongoing at Schoodic Institute in partnership with Park
staff and university and other nonprofit partners is important to the
Park's improving its resilience to the impacts of the changing climate.
Thanks to Acadia's superb science coordinator, Dr. Abe Miller-Rush-
ing, I have learned much about ecological changes in Acadia. The Park
has the great good fortune to possess a treasure trove of old records of
observations by expert naturalists. Acadia knows that it has lost over
200 plant species in the past century, and about one-quarter of its plants
today are not native. Wildlife is changing too with some species disap-
pearing and others arriving. So-called ecological mismatches are being
studied and generate concern—for example, the arrival of birds earlier

in the season before plant and insect foods on which they depend are available. The forests of Acadia lie at the transition from southern hardwood forests to northern coniferous forests and are rich in biodiversity. The iconic forests are going to keep evolving in new ways, hastened by mankind's ongoing damage to the atmosphere.

I find the changing ecosystems of Acadia fascinating despite those changes causing concern and indicating issues that must be addressed. Acadia is a source of great intellectual interest and stimulation even as it remains a favorite locale for outdoor fun and nature observation. Combining all that with fine friendships and a window on National Park Service management and policies has been hugely rewarding. I have been truly privileged to live for so long next to one of the very finest examples of "America's Best Idea."

Early postcard view down our hillside to Center Harbor
and islands beyond—"home of my soul."

Author at tiller of Brutal Beast *Tubby*, 1958. Boats like these,
easily beached on islands, taught the joys of exploring the Maine coast.

Gordon Ambach

Author and father, German H. H. Emory,
on Eggemoggin Reach aboard family's *Arcturus*, 1964.

Half model of Samuel Crocker-designed New Bedford 35 *Arcturus*.

Art Forms to Rejuvenate the Spirit:
Magnificent Landscapes and Lovely Boats

Lisa Heyward

Open their eyes to nature as early as possible!
Acadia National Park across Frenchman Bay.

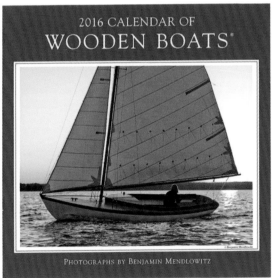

Courtesy of NOAH Publications

Author's Nathanael Herreshoff–designed and -built (1925)
Fish class sloop *Perch*.

"Eggemoggin" being painted on International 500
in preparation for 1970 coastal conservation cruise.

Family time in Cape Breton Island's Bras d'Or Lakes
aboard Bermuda 40 *Eggemoggin*, 1975.

Meadow Brook Farm's 1792 house with modern room
replacing attached derelict barn.

Beavers maintained prehistoric Meadow Brook canoeway
connecting Penobscot and Blue Hill Bays.

Alison Dibble

Dianna sailing *My Ocean*, the original
Nathanael Herreshoff/Joel White Catspaw Dinghy.

Exploring an estuary in Washington County, up the Englishman River.

A Changing Maine:

Old herring dory behind our barn, never to fish again
as Gulf of Maine changes and fisheries evolve.

Dressed and sprayed against disease-bearing deer ticks, author hiking
in Acadia National Park at Isle au Haut on hot summer day.

West Wind and peapod wait while we hike
The Nature Conservancy's Great Wass Island Preserve.

Future stewards of the Earth—young adventurers
in a Frank Day-built dinghy.

11

PROTECTING BIRD HABITAT

My birding skills are limited, although my knowledge, interest, and ability to identify by sight and sounds have improved considerably over the years, spurred by increased personal engagement in the preservation of bird habitat in Maine. As a child I decided one summer that I would watch and list birds on my grandmother's property in Connecticut. I found a notebook and, in a rarely used cupboard, an old pair of binoculars that had belonged to my long-deceased grandfather. I spent a few mornings beginning my "List"—which probably included little more than robins, sparrows, seagulls, crows, perhaps a cardinal, and, without doubt, the purple martins making their home in the big birdhouse on a high pole behind my swing set. Much as I loved the outdoors, however, and appreciated nature and enjoyed seeing birds, an interest in serious birding did not take hold. I soon put down the notebook and binoculars that boyhood summer.

Now, a lifetime later, I am fascinated by how birding has become one of the fastest-growing outdoor recreations in the United States. Baby boomers have, to use a bird term, flocked to the activity. The sheer numbers of bird-watchers are astonishing—and heart-warming. In 2011 forty-six million Americans called themselves bird-watchers according to a report that year by the United States Fish and Wildlife Service. While most are backyard birders, eighteen million take trips away from home to see birds. The interest in observing birds has become a driving force in the eco-tourism industry around the globe. Eco-tourism may be a double-edged sword creating serious environmental and social problems in some places as well as, in others, relatively benign economic benefits, but the explosion of interest in birding has greatly expanded the numbers of people who take a broad interest in wildlife habitat preservation and, beyond that, environmental protection in general. This is a hugely helpful development. We may hope and reasonably expect that this outdoor interest percolates to the younger generation as well. The future of our planet depends on an environmentally conscious public; birding certainly is a valuable educational tool.

I have also been fascinated to learn how study of birds, their migrations, and behaviors provides information vital to understanding changes in climate. That birds are being heavily impacted by climate change is underscored by what National Audubon president David Yarnold wrote in a 2014 issue of the Society's magazine, "Nearly half of our birds are threatened by climate change, and some may suffer extinction." The ever-growing body of data about birds is yielding crucial insights into the condition of entire ecosystems.

Some of my most satisfying land conservation work took place in the early 1990s when I became deeply immersed in the preservation of seabird nesting islands. Shortly after 1990 Tom Goettel, Refuge Manager of Petit Manan National Wildlife Refuge, met with me and my longtime colleague Caroline Pryor, by then Maine Coast Heritage Trust vice president. Tom asked for the meeting to voice his hope that more effort could be directed to protecting seabird nesting islands.

Although over the years I had participated in the protection of some nesting islands, I had not in my own mind specifically focused on that special subset of Maine's islands. Tom pointed out that 10 percent of Maine's coastal islands are bird nesting islands. Many of these islands are completely or largely bald—that is, grass-covered and often rocky but devoid of trees—making them attractive for birds that nest in colonies on the ground such as terns, gulls, cormorants, and eider ducks. Other nesting islands are treed, mostly with spruce and fir along the more eastern parts of the coast, and trees provide nesting habitat for bald eagles, ospreys, and great blue herons.

By the time Tom came to see Caroline and me, the United States Fish and Wildlife Service owned a few nesting islands as did the Maine Department of Inland Fisheries and Wildlife, The Nature Conservancy, the National Audubon Society, and the Maine Audubon Society. A few others were privately owned and protected by conservation easements, but the vast majority of nesting islands remained unprotected.

Nesting islands are especially fragile because undue disturbance during nesting season can wipe out a season's production of young birds on an island. As scared parent birds lift off their eggs or young in the nests, predator birds such as black-backed gulls will swoop in for a meal. The most egregious example of destructive disturbance during nesting season of which I am aware occurred on Compass Island in Penobscot Bay some years ago. A film crew using a helicopter to film the lovely old schooners that carry paying passengers on sailing cruises decided to land for lunch on the island. I am told that the extraordinary commotion totally ruined the season's nesting. The helicopter was, of course, an extreme and rare example. Much more common disturbance is from picnickers, often accompanied by unleashed pet dogs. In recent years there have been greatly expanded efforts to educate the heretofore largely ignorant public about the fragility of nesting islands through the use of the media, brochures at marinas, and signs on islands.

When Tom Goettel, Caroline Pryor, and I talked, we had no idea where money might be found to protect nesting islands by purchasing them. Although a few more islands could be protected by persuading generous owners to donate their nesting islands to conservation agencies or to grant conservation easements, we knew that at the scale Tom considered necessary, many islands would have to be purchased.

This initial meeting of the three of us led to several much larger round-table discussions about what might be done. While I may have forgotten some of the organizations participating in these larger meetings, they certainly included the U.S. Fish and Wildlife Service, the Maine Department of Inland Fisheries and Wildlife, Acadia National Park, The Nature Conservancy, Maine Coast Heritage Trust, the Island Institute, and probably the Audubons—both National and Maine. Also represented, by my presence, was The Conservation Fund, for at that time I was the Maine representative for that organization, based in Arlington, Virginia.

In those early meetings we indeed began with no clear idea of how to find the money for island purchases that adequate nesting island conservation made desirable, but in one way or another we found the path to what became a critical source of money to protect such islands.

I went to Washington along with Maine Coast Heritage Trust president
Jay Espy to meet with members of the Maine Congressional delegation
and staff. The key person in the Maine delegation at the time was the
state's powerful senior senator, George Mitchell, who fortuitously was
Senate Majority Leader and served on the Senate Finance Committee.

On one Washington trip I carried along a photograph that seemed
to have significant impact. One of the very most important nesting
islands on the Maine coast is Jordans Delight well downeast in Mil-
bridge, one of the most exposed, outermost islands and lying just east
of Petit Manan Point. On the seaward, southern side is a high cliff while
the only reasonable landing spot—and only in calm weather—is on
the north end. The owner at the time had persuaded the town to issue
a building permit for a boathouse, which he then built atop the cliff.
Given the location as far from the landing spot as it was possible to be,
the structure was hardly intended as a boathouse but rather as a simple
residence with an extraordinary ocean view. Access required traversing
a path the length of the island through the nesting birds.

On one of Dianna's and my sailing cruises past Jordans Delight,
just after construction of this building so greatly decried in the conservation community, we slipped close under the cliff on a calm late
summer afternoon and shot a photograph of the house. Subsequently,
I had a quality enlargement printed and took that to Washington. I
distinctly remember sitting at Senator Mitchell's imposing conference
table with the Senator and Jay Espy and passing that photograph to the
Senator as we summarized the U. S. Fish and Wildlife Service nesting
data for the island. The photograph of the house atop the cliff underscored better than we ever could verbally the threats facing bird nesting
on Maine islands in the absence of adequate protection. Later in the
day, the offices of the rest of the Maine Congressional delegation saw
the photograph too. I cannot really say how important that photograph
was, but what was vitally important was that Senator Mitchell led the
Maine Congressional delegation in supporting and obtaining Congressional appropriations from the Land and Water Conservation Fund for
purchase of seabird nesting islands by Petit Manan National Wildlife
Refuge. The Land and Water Conservation Fund, funded by federal

government offshore oil revenues, has been a critical source of federal dollars for land acquisitions by the Fish and Wildlife Service and the National Park Service.

With federal dollars flowing, The Conservation Fund, with my handling negotiations, began purchasing nesting islands from willing sellers. Our procedures as a nonprofit allowed us to move much more rapidly than could the government bureaucracy of the Fish and Wildlife Service to take advantage of opportunities provided by willing sellers. The Conservation Fund would buy islands to hold until the Fish and Wildlife Service could buy them from The Conservation Fund, an activity known as "pre-acquiring." At that time Maine Coast Heritage Trust did not have the capital to do these preacquisitions, but later, with access to more capital, Maine Coast Heritage Trust replaced The Conservation Fund as the primary pre-acquirer of nesting islands for the National Wildlife Refuge.

My personal involvement in protecting nesting islands stretched over several years of very rewarding work. What especially made it so satisfying was being part of a team of extraordinarily dedicated people who became great friends as we worked toward our common goals. At the U.S. Fish and Wildlife Service two names particularly stand out in my mind in addition to Tom Goettel, to whom I give much credit for launching the stepped-up initiative to protect nesting islands. They are Maggie Anderson, the charismatic, highly energetic then Project Leader at Petit Manan who too soon, for family reasons, moved to a Refuge in Minnesota, literally leaving everyone in tears at a going-away party; and Stu Fefer, who over a long career has guided the Maine Coastal Program of the Fish and Wildlife Service. Stu's program, working in cooperation with the Maine Department of Inland Fisheries and Wildlife, provided a biological ranking of Maine's nesting islands. This invaluable, endlessly consulted list showed data on the number of nesting pair of each species on a given island. Another government employee who has contributed enormously to the protection of nesting islands and to the efforts at that time is Brad Allen, seabird island expert for the Maine Department of Inland Fisheries and Wildlife. Someone from the same department whom we did not see as much but whose data was vital was eagle legend Charlie Todd.

We citizens are fortunate to be served by such capable government personnel who are so committed to their jobs and the natural world. One Fish and Wildlife Service biologist based in another state was famous for exclaiming, "I love my job so much that I would do it for free if the government would just feed me!" In my early years at Maine Coast Heritage Trust, Dick Parks enthusiastically and skillfully handled acquisitions of land and conservation easements for the Department of Inland Fisheries and Wildlife. He told me of the landowner in Boston who kept refusing to sell a parcel of important wildlife habitat. Dick filled a paper grocery bag with money and drove to Boston for another meeting at the landowner's home. When the landowner again expressed reservations about selling, Dick picked up his bag of currency and emptied it all over the kitchen table. "Does this make a difference?" asked Dick. Deal done!

The nonprofit people working on the preservation of seabird islands were wonderful too. The Island Institute's Philip Conkling brought to discussions an ecologist's in-depth knowledge of Maine islands amassed even before he launched the Island Institute. That same organization's Annette Naegel brought to the team effort invaluable natural resource knowledge of islands as well as warm relationships with many island owners. Bruce Kidman of The Nature Conservancy brought skills as a communications and policy expert, and Jay Espy of Maine Coast Heritage Trust proved highly effective in working to maintain the interest and support of the Congressional delegation.

In this several-year effort during which I was personally involved, I actually wore two hats. I represented The Conservation Fund in Maine, handling purchase negotiations on its behalf, and I also assumed the role of Island Coordinator for Maine Coast Heritage Trust in an effort with Jay Espy and others on the staff to strengthen the Trust's over-all island conservation program. Those I have named and others who played vital roles worked together closely on the many facets of the seabird island effort—identifying priorities, communicating with the Congressional delegation, building public understanding and support, and working with landowners.

Not all the nesting island projects on which I worked involved islands destined for government ownership. Stu Fefer of the Fish and Wildlife Service's Coastal Program talked about the "virtual Refuge" of nesting islands. What was and is important is proper protection, not how an individual island is owned. Nesting islands that have been conserved are, in fact, owned by the federal and state governments, by the national and regional nonprofits, and by local land trusts as well as in some cases being privately owned but restricted by conservation easements. As long as protection of the nesting habitat is adequate, the details of ownership are less important.

Perhaps the nesting island project in which I took greatest pride was indeed an addition to the "virtual Refuge" but not to government ownership. Thirty-eight-acre Browney Island, near Jonesport and just west of Great Wass Island, was then ranked as the third most impor-tant eider nesting island in Maine. On behalf of Maine Coast Heritage Trust, I lunched with the owner of Browney Island near his Boston office, and he very generously offered to sell the island for only what he had paid in property taxes over the years, a quite minimal sum relative to its full fair market value. He also said that having been involved in new business ventures, he would very much like to use this near gift to stimulate a young conservation venture rather than have the island go to a government agency. My colleagues and I at Maine Coast Heritage Trust found the money to pay the modest purchase price, and title to the island went to the fledgling local land trust for the area, the Great Auk Land Trust—with great enthusiasm on the part of its president, Robert Miller, who did so much to launch this land trust. Its acquisi-tion of Browney Island proved a very useful expression of confidence in the land trust's future.

Great Auk went on to be the well-respected land trust for the western portion of the Washington County coastline from just east of Schoodic to the Jonesport area. Then it merged with Quoddy Regional Land Trust to become the Downeast Coastal Conservancy and a yet more major player on the coastal conservation scene. At the time of the merger I was asked to join the new board of directors, an invitation that I accepted with particular pleasure because of my earlier Browney Island role.

Dianna and I have snaked our way carefully through surrounding ledges to anchor off Browney Island a couple of times after nesting season was safely over and explored its lovely mix of fields and woods with spectacular views in all directions. Interestingly, although the island was such an important eider nesting island at the time that Great Auk Land Trust acquired it, the population of eiders on that particular island declined dramatically in subsequent years, but at least the island stands as protected nesting island habitat now and in the future for birds of whatever species choose to use it.

My most personal encounter with eiders, the males so gorgeously white and black, is worth recounting, for I have never had a similar experience. One spectacular September day I was sailing home alone from Roque Island, Dianna's having disembarked in Jonesport. Threading the narrow passage between Schoodic Island and Schoodic Point I could see ahead a large raft of eiders. Usually these ducks take flight upon the approach of a boat, but this time, heeled over and traveling fast in the strong breeze, the boat charged right into their midst. Somehow they had not sensed my approach. All around the boat's lifelines were panicked eiders desperately trying to get airborne in a noisy frenzy of white spray and flailing wings.

Farther east than Browney and farther out into the Gulf of Maine is Machias Seal Island. One year Dianna and I sailed to that bird nesting island, the ownership of which is in dispute between the United States and Canada although its management is under Environment Canada. Anchorage and landing are problematic except in a flat calm, and almost all visitors come in a commercial tour boat. Even on the glassy day that we ventured out on our own, the slight swell dropped our dinghy hard onto the flat ledge at the landing spot. The thrill of the birds on the island was worth it, though. Environment Canada maintains wooden boardwalks for visitors so that they stay clear of nests. Walking across the island on the boardwalks, we kept our hands on our heads to ward off the cacophonous, constant dive-bombing attacks of clouds of terns. Most fascinating was sitting in a blind and watching puffins, which I had first seen on a sailing approach to the cliffs of Grand Manan.

In this century tragedy struck Machias Seal Island in what may be a canary-in-the-coal-mine warning for all of us. The nesting terns, Arctic and common, abandoned Machias Seal in 2005 according to Linda Welch, U.S. Fish and Wildlife Service biologist, and through 2014 did not produce a single chick there. By 2016 a few pairs struggled to reestablish themselves, 175 pairs versus the approximately 3,500 pairs that once nested on the island. Lack of food off eastern Maine, especially herring, caused by changes in the Gulf of Maine resulted in the complete collapse of what had been the largest tern colony in the region. Gull predation may be hindering the recovery, according to Linda.

Northern gannets are a favorite bird to see on our cruises to the east of Schoodic Point. They rarely come up into Maine's bays, but we do occasionally see them off the outer edges of land west of Schoodic too. So white, so large, so streamlined in appearance with their slim bodies and long, thin wings, and so graceful in flight—the enjoyment of watching them soaring in flight and sitting on the water provides good reason to venture along the outermost coast. We have a starkly white fiberglass peapod rowboat built by Brooklin's Eric Dow, which we named *Gannet* to remind us of these magnificent birds.

Like the terns, gannets are in trouble. Nesting not in Maine but far to the north in Newfoundland, Labrador, and the Gulf of St. Lawrence region of Quebec, gannets in large numbers in 2012 and 2014 reportedly abandoned nests in Newfoundland, leaving chicks to starve. The suspected cause is that in those years water temperatures were significantly above normal, causing the usual food fish of gannets to move away to find colder waters. A 2014 National Audubon Society report on climate change lists gannets as one of the bird species most at risk of losing suitable breeding sites.

The work with nesting islands certainly whetted my interest in preserving bird habitat, and my activities in that regard have spanned other
types of bird habitat, too. During my time representing The Conservation Fund in the early 1990s, I negotiated an addition to the Petit
Manan National Wildlife Refuge known as Williams Point, a forested
parcel with extensive salt marsh on Gouldsboro's West Bay. With subsequent additions the Williams Point acreage came to about 400 acres.
A decade later I discovered that the adjacent 400 acres of forest was on
the market. Combined, the two parcels would provide about 800 acres
of forested habitat.

The U.S. Fish and Wildlife Service had neither funds nor authority to buy the additional 400 acres, but the refuge manager at the
time, Charlie Blair, strongly encouraged me to try to find a conservation owner and the funds for the purchase. He emphasized that it
was getting harder and harder to keep relatively large forested acreages
along the coast unfragmented. Large acreages of unfragmented forest
are critical, he underscored, to bird species that nest in forest interi-
ors, not near the edges—for example, the wood thrush, a Neotropical
migrant which, according to the Cornell Laboratory of Ornithology,
has declined more than 50 percent since 1966. Because of the tie that
I already felt to Williams Point, I pursued this possibility with enthusiasm. The local land trust for eastern Hancock County, Frenchman
Bay Conservancy, agreed to own and manage the property, and Dianna
and I led the effort to put together the necessary funds. To our great
pleasure we succeeded.

I chuckled at one of the foundation proposals we submitted when
seeking the funds for that Frenchman Bay Conservancy land purchase.
On the day before Thanksgiving I had been exploring the property
and encountered a bull moose in a small pond in the forest. One of
the foundations to which we were applying for a grant was particularly interested in funding land conservation projects benefiting a wide
variety of wildlife. Dianna and I were back on the property on our skis
a couple of months after my moose encounter, and while we did not

see a moose, we saw substantial piles of moose droppings, which we photographed where they sat on the sunlit snow. We included the best of those photographs in the grant request to that foundation, wondering whether the foundation had ever before found photos of poop in a proposal to it.

By the time we achieved our goal with the forested parcel in Gouldsboro and saw it safely in the hands of Frenchman Bay Conservancy, Dianna and I had already worked with another local land trust, Blue Hill Heritage Trust, to conserve a different type of bird habitat— hayfields and freshwater wetlands, which are vital to several Neotropical migratory species that nest in such open areas. Our own acquisition of Meadow Brook Farm in Sedgwick in 2002 was our most personal venture into conserving land and led to a major new facet in our lives.

12

MEADOW BROOK FARM

I t all started with a hilarious canoe voyage, if "voyage" can refer to threading a canoe on foot through tightly packed spruce trees and climbing them to search for a more open route. The story of Dianna's and my stewardship of a Sedgwick heirloom, Meadow Brook Farm, could be said to begin with my father's persuading me in the early 1960s that Brooklin is an island, surrounded by the waters of Blue Hill Bay, Eggemoggin Reach, the Benjamin River, Meadow Brook, and the Salt Pond. Bent on circumnavigation, two brothers-in-law and I headed up the Benjamin River in a brand-new, green-painted aluminum canoe.

Dad had some historical justification for what he said, but I don't know where he had been since well before 1876. In that year a Reverend Fish gave a July 4th address in which he stated, ". . . it is said that at certain early times boats could pass entirely around the present town of Brooklin. . . ." For Native Americans the protected route connecting Eggemoggin Reach to Blue Hill Bay was likely maintained as a water highway by beavers building dams. At any rate, the three of us, with the canoe, eventually emerged from woods north of the Benjamin River into Great Meadow. We then dragged and stumbled over ankle-twisting, hummocky ground hidden by waist-high grasses, came to Meadow Brook, which divides Brooklin from Sedgwick, and gratefully resumed paddling. That new green paint had largely been left on the spruce branches. No, Dad, Brooklin is not an island.

Nearly forty years later in 2002 I was serving on the board of directors of Blue Hill Heritage Trust, the local land trust for the six towns on the Blue Hill Peninsula including Brooklin and Sedgwick. Early on a rainy, cold June morning we on the executive committee gathered for what we anticipated to be a discussion of routine Trust affairs. The unscheduled first order of business launched for Dianna and me a personal conservation project that has rewarded and educated us in ways that we treasure. High-quality habitat for bobolinks, harriers, bitterns, woodcock, and a host of other bird species has been conserved. Scenic roadside vistas have been preserved, and working hayfields supplying local hay markets will never be destroyed by buildings and pavement. An historic farmhouse still looms alone in its pastoral and wooded setting, unmarred by inappropriate neighboring development that could so easily have arisen.

As we executive committee members settled ourselves around the conference table in the tiny upstairs room in Blue Hill Heritage Trust's simple office, board members Peter Clapp, owner and operator of the Blue Hill Garage, and Pam Johnson, operator of her own gardening business in the town of Sedgwick, asked to discuss an opportunity and threat that Peter had been following closely. Recently deceased was Gordon Campbell, the aged owner of Sedgwick's Meadow Brook Farm, also known as Punchbowl Farm—95 acres of hayfields, freshwater wetland meadows, and forest.

Peter had just been called by a realtor with word that the executors of the estate were about to list the property for sale but might consider a reasonable offer from the land trust before advertising the farm. Peter and Pam were persuasive as to the conservation values of the farm and the very real threat in the then active real estate market of subdivision into numerous house lots. Tackling such threats to properties with exceptional conservation values is the *raison d'etre* of land trusts. The opportunity might be fleeting, said Peter and Pam, and we should look for a way to seize it.

By total coincidence as to timing, Dianna and I had spent that spring looking for a property in which we could indulge our passion for conserving natural lands. Having worked for so long in the land conservation arena, I was intrigued by the possibility of finding a personal land conservation project—one that might combine a reasonable long-term investment prospect with the immediate possibility of permanently preserving vital natural attributes. When I heard about the availability of Meadow Brook Farm and knowing the very limited financial capability of Blue Hill Heritage Trust at that time to act quickly on its own, I immediately sensed an opportunity to facilitate the Trust's achieving the habitat protection that Peter and Pam sought.

No sooner had the morning's meeting adjourned than Pam and I along with board president Alison Dibble, a professional botanist, and executive director Jim Dow, an attorney by training with long experience in environmental and conservation work, headed out through the dreary rain to Meadow Brook Farm. Although I had driven by the property occasionally my whole life, I saw it through new eyes that day, and it took little imagination looking out over the vast hayfield and wetland meadow complex to comprehend the conservation significance of the property. As we stood in a chilly downpour at the edge of the road, we gazed out over an exquisite mix of yellow buttercups and white daisies, and, in the wetter areas, vast lavender carpets of wild iris. Never had I seen iris in such profusion.

I made a proposal to my compatriots: Dianna and I would make an immediate attempt to buy the farm. If successful, we would give Blue Hill Heritage Trust a year-long option to buy the property from us at our cost, and we would contribute back part of what they would pay us. If after analysis the board of directors preferred not to buy and thereby burden the Trust with owning and managing the property, we would donate to the Trust a very restrictive conservation easement. The board could use the coming months to evaluate both alternatives and tell us which worked best for the Trust. I would recuse myself from that decision process.

By afternoon I had heard Dianna exclaim on the telephone, "Oh my god, that is the property I've been saying for years that I love so much and should be preserved." She had biked by many times on frequent excursions from our house in Brooklin, just six miles away. By the end of the afternoon, following a meeting of Jim Dow and me with the realtor, the realtor had an offer from Dianna and me on its way to the children of the deceased owner, an offer they rapidly accepted.

A great personal adventure for Dianna and me was underway, and the initiative and dedication of Pam and Peter had already paid off in buying time for the Trust to work with us to find the best permanent conservation solution for the pastoral and wildlife treasure—cultural treasure too—that is Meadow Brook Farm. The conservation solution that ultimately was chosen was our retaining ownership and granting Blue Hill Heritage Trust a conservation easement.

⚜

Meadow Brook Farm straddles Route 172 six miles south of Blue Hill village and two miles north of Sedgwick village. From the road 68 acres of sloping hayfields, wetland meadows, and forest sweep southeastward to the edge of Meadow Brook just a short distance south of where it flows into the Salt Pond. The hayfields are cut by a second brook, Thurston Brook, named for the family that bought our farm in 1796 and farmed it until the early 1900s. That brook comes under the road and meanders among alders until it empties into Meadow Brook. Meadow Brook drains an extensive freshwater wetland known as Great Meadow, which extends southerly almost to the upper reaches of the Benjamin River.

Another 27 acres of the farm lie directly across Route 172 and rise relatively steeply from the road. Near the top of the slope the farm abuts several hundred acres of commercial blueberry barrens rolling off to the northward and interspersed with woods and wetlands. At the end of a small hayfield by the road stands the colonial-style post-and-beam farmhouse constructed by Benjamin Friend in 1792. Most of the rest of the land on this side of the road is now wooded as long-abandoned, rocky sheep pastures revert first to hardwood and, increasingly, to conifers, but in the most northerly corner, hidden and secretive in its isolation and access, is one more small field. Stone walls, which once fenced the pastures, still course through the woods.

The neighborhood remains pastoral and rural. To the immediate south of us on both sides of the road is an even larger former farm, now almost all overgrown. Decay and fire have taken down the buildings. Elsewhere, numerous open fields remain. The wood frame houses, often with remaining barns and sheds in various stages of maintenance and deterioration, are typical of New England. Some of the neighbors have been in Sedgwick for generations. Others are much more recent arrivals. Some work at a variety of jobs—on the land or in nearby towns.

Some are retirees, and others only appear during vacations. While the character is remarkably pastoral and to some degree still agricultural, boats are seen in many yards during the winter, for this is coastal Maine with Eggemoggin Reach and Blue Hill Bay close by.

Down the road from Meadow Brook Farm about a mile toward Brooklin were other active farms when I was growing up. In their barn Mrs. Cousins sold fresh vegetables she and her husband raised in the back field, and she greeted one and all with a warm smile. Nearly next door, Mrs. Belfay sold fresh eggs and chicken from her henhouse. My grandmother and mother were regular customers at both farms, and often I rode along with them on their food-shopping forays. Occasionally, my cousins and I were allowed to play in the Cousinses' hayloft while our elders made their purchases. These small farms along Route 172 have always been a treasured memory of childhood summer days.

My grandmother Dodi was a bit of a character and loved nothing more in the summer than to surround herself with grandchildren. Many of us would gather around her table at lunch, and frequently the primary dish was one of Mrs. Belfay's capons. Male cousins and I loved asking as the chicken was served, "Dodi, what is a capon?" She would flash her amused smile and tolerantly respond, "A rooster that's been diddled with!" Great guffaws of appreciative laughter always followed.

The single most important conservation value of Meadow Brook Farm is the bird habitat in its hayfields and freshwater wetlands. Wildlife specialists talk of "focus species," the most important species of wildlife for which a property might be managed. Managing for selected focus species should not only result in maximizing the habitat values for those species but also provide good habitat for associated species within the particular ecosystem. At Meadow Brook Farm a focus species clearly should be bobolinks.

I did not even know what a bobolink looks like that dreary morning when I decided to try to buy the property, but in making the case for its preservation other Blue Hill Heritage Trust board members with more extensive wildlife knowledge pointed out that the farm provides considerable nesting habitat for bobolinks, which are frequently sighted in its fields. My colleagues explained that these birds are in decline and merit efforts to preserve their habitat.

The uniquely colored male in breeding plumage is black on the underside with white on the tops of the wings and on the rump. Especially distinctive is the buff color (almost yellow) on the back of the head. The brownish coloring of the females and juveniles and, indeed, of the males too by fall, lacks such drama, but as equally captivating as the black, white, and buff of the breeding males is the species' cheery and bubbling *bob-o-link* song. I have come to take special pleasure in listening for the bobolinks and in looking for them flying over the fields or, where I most often see them, perching on the tall, shrubby growth where the hayfield merges into the wetland meadow.

The grassland prairies of the Midwest were the native breeding habitat for bobolinks, but the prairies' destruction by agriculture forced bobolinks to look to hayfields for their preferred nesting habitat. To quote from "Eastern Bobolink populations: Ecology and conservation in an agricultural landscape" by Bollinger and Gavin in *Ecology and Conservation of Neotropical Migrant Landbirds*, "Hayfields currently are one of the largest blocks of suitable nesting habitat for Bobolinks in the eastern United States. . . 'Old' hayfields . . . [are] especially preferred by Bobolinks and appear to represent optimum habitat." By "old hayfield" they mean fields left for years without crop rotation or reseeding. The authors of this study also reported that hayfield size is important to the number of bobolinks in a field, the abundance increasing exponentially with field size. For coastal Maine our farm's relatively large hayfields, untouched for years except for one annual mowing, provide ideal habitat, a fact in which we take considerable pleasure and pride.

A major danger to bobolink breeding success and to other species of grassland nesting birds is mowing hayfields too early in the season before the young have fledged. There are two major pressures to mow early. One is to be able to harvest more than one crop of hay per season. The other is that early hay provides the most nutritious animal feed, this latter fact first told me by Maine's great agricultural conservationist

Paul Birdsall of nearby Penobscot, whose organic farm's name, Horse-power Farm, explains his attention to the nutritional qualities of hay. He needs top-quality hay to keep his draft horses healthy. Because we have given the highest priority at Meadow Brook Farm to preserving wildlife habitat values, we included in the conservation easement we granted a provision prohibiting mowing before July 15. This date was suggested by Maine Audubon as one that would protect most of the birds. We did not want to be so restrictive about cutting the hay that we might find it hard to find someone to mow. I am very glad that in practice our Sedgwick neighbor Bruce Grindal, whom we let have the hay in return for mowing, also is in the blueberry business and does most of the mowing beginning at the end of August after the blueberry harvest—and after all young birds have fledged.

We may be doing our best to take care of "our" bobolinks during the late spring and summer, but what, I have wondered, happens to them when in the fall they depart the sanctuary of Meadow Brook Farm? They are truly one of the most long-distance of the so-called Neo-tropical migrants. Their winter grounds are on the vast grasslands and farm fields of Argentina as well as in neighboring countries including Paraguay and Bolivia. There birds that during the summer are widely dispersed over large parts of North America congregate in huge, hungry flocks, which can decimate grain crops. The guns of angry Argentine farmers and toxins applied in Latin American agriculture must take a terrible toll.

We became so enamored of bobolinks through owning Meadow Brook Farm that when we had a 30-foot, cat-ketch-rigged, round-bilged sharpie sailboat built in 2012, we named her *Bobolink*. It just seemed appropriate given her black carbon spars and light yellow topsides. When we were on her far away, the name was a fun reminder of the lovely farm back in Sedgwick.

Bobolinks may be a focus species in managing the fields of Meadow Brook Farm, but the wide variety of birdlife has been one of the great pleasures of becoming acquainted with this property. Other grassland and wetland meadow birds are common. In the summer I can hardly swing my binoculars over the wetland meadows looking for bobolinks without seeing red-winged blackbirds perching and flying over Great Meadow. In and over the growing hay are savannah sparrows, and earlier, when the new season's grass is just beginning to turn green and grow, bitterns come up from their usual haunt in the wet areas to stalk slowly across the drier fields, bending their long necks to feed. At dusk in the spring we often hear the peculiar *thunk* sound of the bitterns. On the taller branches of the alders along Thurston Brook, the flashing brightness of male goldfinches is a frequent sight.

Harriers, or marsh hawks as they also are called, a light-colored, large gray hawk, can often be seen hunting low over the fields. One and possibly two pair are reported to nest on neighboring land. Turkey vultures sometimes soar high overhead, and wild turkeys occasionally descend into the fields in large flocks. I once counted twenty-three in the field next to the house.

Ducks, snipes, swifts, woodpeckers, warblers, and woodcock—they and the other species one would expect on a coastal Maine farm are all here. What we most especially welcome back each spring are the phoebes which nest under overhangs on the house. Their early arrival in March, often with snow still covering the ground, provides welcome reassurance that winter will indeed finally end.

The most unusual bird event was the visit over a period of about ten days in April 2007 of a lone sandhill crane. Local birder Chip Mosely even was able to photograph it, and both Dianna and I were thrilled when we each caught sight of it standing in the wetland and flying low over the marsh. At the time I had no idea that sandhill cranes ever appeared in the East, but although unusual in our part of Maine, they are occasionally sighted and may be nesting farther south in the state.

The readily apparent conservation values of Meadow Brook Farm encouraged us to dig more deeply into its natural significance. We commissioned our professional botanist friend Alison Dibble to prepare a natural resources inventory. Not only did she confirm the interesting ornithological aspects with a list of 114 bird species sighted over a four-and-a-half-year period by credible observers, but she gave us very interesting perspective on the vegetation and diversity of plants. Although no rare plants were found among the high species richness of 237 species, some she said are rare in the area. She reported that our patches of ragged-fringed orchids in the hayfields were the largest, most vigorous she has seen in Hancock County and indicate especially high-quality habitat. She also commented that lichens and bryophytes are especially diverse at the farm due to the clean air and the farm's wide variety of habitats and substrates. Alison was excited by finding one lichen that she had never before seen despite having looked for it throughout the area. In the farm's woods she found some trees of unusually large diameter for a region where woodlots were cut repeatedly following European settlement.

Apple trees grow in many places on the farm. An autumnal delight is tasting them all and returning time and again to the trees with the most pleasing fruit.

With our interest in protecting wildlife habitat, we have been pleased that the farm is a site of habitation or visitation for many mammals. One July 4th morning we were eating breakfast when Dianna whispered, "Very slowly turn around and look out the door behind you." There ambling across the grass was a female black bear. A year or two earlier out the same door Dianna spotted a bobcat on top of a ledge behind the lawn. There has been a coyote den in the woods behind the house at least some winters. Beavers are a constant presence in Meadow and Thurston brooks. Each brook has a lodge. We rarely see the beavers, but we see their dams, paths on stream banks, and the astonishing results of their removal of saplings and small trees.

By buying Meadow Brook Farm we truly bought into a Sedgwick legacy. In 1796 Benjamin Friend sold his four-year-old farmhouse with its surrounding acreage to David Thurston. His heirs report that Thurston brought his family, worldly goods, and livestock by ship to the reversing Blue Hill Falls where the Salt Pond meets Blue Hill Bay. He then barged them up the Salt Pond to his new farm. Meadow Brook Farm was to remain in possession of Thurston descendants for over a century until John Thurston finally sold it in 1928.

The farm is rife with history. Presumably, Thurstons were the ones who built the impressive stone mill dam, the remains of which still span the brook that bears their name and forms the northeastern boundary of the farm north of the state highway. We have been told that at some point when there still was a pond behind the dam, an owner stocked it with fish and charged tourists for the privilege of fishing in it. A dramatic piece of reported farm history is that about 1948 in the early days of jet-powered aviation an Air Force fighter jet flying from Bangor crash-landed in a low area in the field and skidded uphill across the field before coming to a stop just short of the huge barn. Today that barn and its silo lie as a heap of rubble, but I can remember when it still stood very close to the edge of Route 172, one of the largest barns in the county. Photographs we have been given show a sign on the barn saying "1916." Even more interesting is a photograph showing on the same site a prior, very large complex of barn buildings.

The old house is remarkable for 1792. With its 1,200-square-foot footprint, two floors, and huge attic, it must have been a large house for that era. Its colonial-style proportions are most pleasing and the posts and beams massive.

When we purchased the farm, the house was a cosmetic mess but fortunately structurally sound with new roof shingles. It had been changed many times over the years, which, although perhaps not what historic preservation aficionados would prefer, demonstrates a dynamism over time that kept it functional for its owners' changing needs and increased comfort. The massive original center chimney with four fireplaces is gone, although three of the lovely old fireplace surrounds and mantles survive.

The combination of field stone, bricks, and concrete in the basement walls and a concrete, if deteriorating, basement floor all show that work under the house took place at different times. I had viewed the basement as a damp, unappealing place, and its spiders keep Dianna completely out. I was most amused, therefore, when Thurston descendant and local historic preservation expert Fred Marston went down and exclaimed, "Oh, a basement to die for!" Sometimes through ignorance we overlook our own treasures, and my attitude toward the basement has been much more positive ever since—although Dianna's attitude about the spiders remains firm.

Of course, indoor plumbing and electricity had long ago been added as well as central oil-fired baseboard heating for parts of the house. With massive cleanup, paint, and some relatively minor repairs and rewiring, the house was usable, comfortable, and enjoyable for us, although several years after purchase we vastly improved it by adding a new living room with dining area and modernized kitchen. The upstairs ceilings are low, a common feature of early New England houses, but even though I am tall, after years on sailboats and a destroyer I am used to ducking my head and actually enjoy the ceilings' and door frames' reminder of times past.

Although the house is not in original condition, we did want to explore its historical significance and were privileged that experts from both Historic New England and the Maine Historic Preservation Commission wanted to look at it. Their advice about its unusual features, its historically important characteristics, and how to care for it in regard to matters such as drainage around the foundation were both fascinating and helpful. The most significant artifact in the house is what was probably the original front door, removed and placed in the attic long ago. The latch is made of wood and has survived because it was taken out of the weather before it could rot away. Such wooden latches as remain, we were told, are rare.

We considered the possibility of granting an historic preservation easement on the house in addition to granting conservation easements on the land. The house might have merited it despite the changes over the years, for its original exterior appearance seemed to be intact, and the way it sits in the landscape demonstrates the ability of early farmers to site their houses superbly. I was familiar with historic preservation easements from having been involved, when executive director of the Land Trust Exchange, in co-publishing with the National Trust for Historic Preservation a booklet on how to appraise properly the impact on a property's fair market value of a conservation easement on land or an historic preservation easement on a building.

We made contact with Maine Preservation, which holds such

historic preservation easements, about the possibility, but we were deterred by the facts that the house was no museum of originality and that Maine Preservation would require a hefty cash contribution to endow future costs of monitoring and enforcing the easement. Also, adding to the cost and burden of such an historic preservation easement on the building would be mandatory maintenance requirements and limitations on changes that might otherwise be desirable.

In a way, I was disappointed that pursuing an historic preservation easement seemed not to make sense for our situation. I have long thought that there could be benefits to communities in establishing closer ties between land conservation and historic preservation efforts, and I had thought that we might have a good opportunity for a demonstration project. Historic preservation societies, at least in Maine's small towns, seem to be largely energized by very community-minded elders, usually of local descent. The people behind land conservation efforts more typically span a wider range of ages and include a higher proportion of people who have moved to the area from elsewhere or are summer residents. Also, land conservation efforts often have greater access to funding. Because both endeavors, preserving a community's historic structures and protecting a community's scenic landscapes, ecological systems, and working farms and forests, are vital to preserving community pride and character, it only makes sense to try to gain the synergy that should be possible by establishing strong ties between the two undertakings.

❧

When we bought the house, it had an attached barn, which was probably 100 years newer than the house and stick-built, not post-and-beam like the house. It was in far worse condition than the house, however, and when we discovered that it would cost more to restore than replace, we had it torn down.

The barn had spoken powerfully to Meadow Brook Farm's agricultural past. Inside was a large walk-in refrigerator, many bins for storing produce, and a summer kitchen with a large sink for washing vegetables and slaughtered livestock. The children of the deceased owner just prior to us told us that their father had at one time kept many thousands of young chickens in the huge barn across the road, being raised to sell to other farms, and a hundred sheep in the rocky hillside pastures on the north side of the property, pastures now largely reverted to early successional forest growth. Cows, sometimes belonging to other farmers who paid for their pasturage, grazed in the large hayfields, and an extensive area of terraces at one end of a field with very deep and fertile soils reportedly had chicken houses and later was used for strawberries. An old galvanized pipe coming down the hillside from a small pond at the top of the rise indicates that water was available where the terraces are.

Dianna and I have not had time nor inclination to try to turn ourselves into farmers, but she has taken advantage of good soils and exposure for outstanding flower gardens. I have enjoyed extracting old but productive grapevines from an apple tree and getting them established on wires, where they are much easier of access. In the winters I have pruned the vines based on instructions found on the web, and I have followed the advice of one of Australia's largest vintners, with whom I happened to spend an afternoon, to bury portions of the long vines after pulling them from the apple tree in order to foster root growth closer to where new growth and grape development take place. The hay that Bruce Grindal takes from the fields goes to animal feed and blueberry barren burning, so that also continues the agricultural tradition of Meadow Brook Farm.

An unintended crop we discovered hidden in one of our areas of puckerbrush was marijuana. What I first spotted one day was a garden hose in a most unlikely place, which I followed to a nearby brook, where I found a 12-volt boat bilge pump that clearly had been attached to a car battery. I found multiple small cleared and carefully cultivated areas near the outlet end of the hose. One family response to my expressed concern was, "Oh, Dad, in this day and age that is like being worried about someone raising roses," but my attorney thought otherwise. To protect myself I absolutely needed to report it, he advised. The Drug Enforcement Agency official to whom I talked said that they would keep an eye on it from their helicopter, but I have no idea whether they ever did. The crop had already been harvested when I stumbled on the patches, and I had torn them up and removed the hose to show that they had been discovered. It was several years before they reappeared. Having a very good guess as to who our trespassing "guerilla grower" was, I simply talked to his girlfriend and probable co-cultivator rather than again involving law enforcement. The plants were gone by the next day and, to my knowledge, for good.

Meadow Brook Farm has been extremely satisfying and educational. We have learned much about birds and mammals, forests, wetlands, vernal pools, lichens and mosses, and old houses. The conservation of its scenic, agricultural, and habitat qualities probably would not have happened without our purchase. At that time, before the Great Recession, the market for subdivision for houses was in a very active state.

The thanks we continue to receive for conserving it and the ongoing occasional requests from Downeast Audubon and other organizations to lead bird trips in our fields reinforce our being glad that we moved quickly that cold, rainy June day in 2002.

13

WOODEN BOATS—AN ART FORM
OF PROFOUND GENIUS

Meadow Brook Farm took us to the convergence of land conservation and historic preservation. Devotion to community is vital
to quality of life in Maine coastal towns—and most everywhere else
too. Preserving important natural characteristics of the landscape *and*
preserving the best of a community's architectural heritage greatly but-
tress devotion to community, which enhances stability, security, health,
and satisfaction in daily lives. For some years I served on an historic
preservation grants committee of the Maine Community Foundation.
Reviewing proposals for restoring fine old buildings greatly expanded
my appreciation of architectural preservation, what it involves, and the
benefits.

Do fine old boats merit the same attention as historic houses? May
they also be cultural treasures? Certainly the constituency for preservation of old boats is far smaller than for old buildings, but I listen
carefully to the words of my friend Jon Wilson, founder of *Wooden-
Boat* magazine and once a wooden boat builder himself. Says Jon in a
wonderful film entitled *Wood, Sails, Dreams,* for which he is the lead
narrator, ". . . the genius that went into the design and construction of
some of these yachts and boats is so profound that it deserves the kind
of recognition that we are used to in architectural preservation." Jon
continues, "Something should be done to save this art form. They are
beautiful creations."

I have not matched Jon's commitment to wooden boats. The cruising boat of Jon and his wife Sherry is a wooden Concordia cutter maintained immaculately. Since selling my wooden International 500 yawl
Eggemoggin in the long ago of 1974, I have only bought fiberglass cruising boats—all of outstanding design, only one of which was of less-
than-excellent-quality construction. Much as I look back with nostalgia

at my years in wooden boats and recall with pleasure the aesthetics of their looks and smells and how they move through the water, I have not missed the costs of properly maintaining them, nor in bad weather at sea have I missed their often greater fragility.

I recall clearly in the 1966 Transatlantic Race from Bermuda to Copenhagen in *Adele* running in near-gale conditions under spinnaker through thick fog day and night across the Grand Banks southeast of Newfoundland. Off watch I would lie in the bunk and think, "Thank god if we collide with one of the innumerable fishing boats out here, our hull is made of steel." In such a nightmare scenario the steel of that Ted Hood–designed, Dutch-built yawl might only have dented whereas a wooden hull, no matter how stout, might have received crushed frames and planks and rapidly sunk. I had twice witnessed how a wooden boat's planking can be broken inwards—once on a Herreshoff 12½ when we hit the corner of a float and, more dramatically, crewing in a very light-air race on the wonderful big yawl *Temptation* when Nantucket Sound current pushed us into the steel lifting pad-eye of a large navigation buoy.

Although fiberglass is not as strong as steel and can be torn and punctured, for sure, there are no seams to open up, and it can tolerate mediocre maintenance far better than wood. Back and forth to the Canadian Maritimes, the Caribbean, Bermuda, and the Bahamas in my own boats and skirting and even hitting the dangerous ledges of Maine, I have taken comfort in the seemingly greater ultimate safety of sound fiberglass construction. Owning a large wooden boat today requires either a great deal of time, patience, and skill if one does the maintenance oneself, or an ability and willingness to pay yard bills exponentially higher than in pre-fiberglass eras for painting, varnishing, and the occasional inevitable replacement of deteriorating wood and fastenings.

Beautiful wooden boats do cast their spell upon me, though. I feast my eyes on the gorgeous wooden boats that grace Brooklin's Center Harbor. I row around them endlessly, and now that I stand-up paddleboard too, I look right into their cockpits and peer through their companionways. I totally agree with Jon that fine wooden boats are an art form as significant as beautiful buildings, fine furniture, or exceptionally crafted wooden musical instruments. The shapes of superbly designed wooden hulls, the enhancement of their shapes by skilled application of varnish and paint, and the visual appearance of structural elements and fine craftsmanship reward my eye and my brain's pleasure sensors beyond any other form of art.

The case has been made that art is therapeutic for the soul. My psyche's response to the intense beauty of great wooden sailboats is a renewal of cheerfulness and optimism as antidote to frequently despairing about the state of our world and society. Parallel to my two passions of sailing and conservation are similar responses to the beauties of fine boats and the gorgeousness of Maine's coastal landscapes.

I have wrestled, especially in recent years, with the question of whether to engage in the preservation of this art form, given my lifelong fascination with boats. In Ivor Wilkins's magnificently produced, huge book *Classic: The Revival of Classic Boating in New Zealand,* he reports asking a major proponent of restoring great wooden vessels, "What is it . . . that motivates such dedication to preserving yachts from yesteryear?" The answer he received: "In a word, madness." Many people have obviously recognized the mad aspects yet fortunately plunged ahead with the challenges and rewards of restoring wooden boats to the benefit of the larger group that cherishes them.

To me it is very much a matter of scale and financial constraints and priorities. With all the rowing that I do and all the towing of a rowboat to get ashore when cruising, I very much favor wooden ones. Good wooden rowboats are lovely and in use provide great aesthetic reward; they feel more solid in the water; and when scraped landing on ledges and rocky beaches, a wooden boat's scars from such use can be easily puttied and repainted for the next season. I can cope myself with the springtime ritual of painting and varnishing on boats of rowboat size and, indeed, enjoy doing that annual maintenance. Skilled repairs are needed only rarely, and when necessary I have found hiring expert boat carpenters to replace or refasten planks or repair broken frames on these small boats affordable, if not cheap.

My exit from personal responsibility for wooden boats resulted not only from the sale of my first *Eggemoggin* but also by the later sale of the family's wooden Herreshoff 12 ½ and a Beetle Cat I had purchased when my children were of an age for that class of small boat. That left me with only the wooden rowboats. I have had no end of pleasure from the fiberglass replacements for the smaller sailboats—a Cape Cod Bulls Eye, which is to the same Herreshoff hull design as the original 12 ½s, and a British Uffa Fox–designed Flying 15, one of the earlier planing keel boat designs. I paint the bottoms of these fiberglass sailboats myself, clean and wax or paint the topsides, and do other minor maintenance, as needed. Why on earth would I go back to the greater time and financial commitment that a wooden sailboat, even a small daysailer, would require?

Out of the blue in 2009 came a telephone call that by 2013 would result in my giving a huge amount of thought to the possibility of acquiring a wooden daysailer needing a complete restoration to be usable. At the time all I knew about the caller, Alec Brainerd, was that he was a respected young boatbuilder in Rockport, Maine. I did remember that his grandfather John Brainerd, a retired biology professor dedicated to conserving the natural qualities of his beloved Penobscot Bay area, had been on the board of directors of Blue Hill Heritage Trust with me in my early years on that board. I knew too that Alec's father Roger at one time skippered the big fisherman-style schooner *Nathaniel Bowditch*. I recalled John fondly and was delighted to chat with Alec, who certainly springs from a heritage with great nature preservation and maritime credentials. The focus of Alec's own interests and endeavors I quickly learned is restoration of fine old wooden boats, construction of replicas, and preservation of the necessary skills.

Alec got directly to the point. In Connecticut had been found my father's old Herreshoff Fish-class sloop, or "Fish Boat," a 16-foot-on-the-waterline design that was an enlarged version of the Herreshoff 12 ½ and, in fact, even prettier because of Herreshoff's stretching out the bow profile. Writing of the iconic, lovely Fish class in a letter dated 1970, Nathanael Herreshoff's son, L. Francis Herreshoff, another superstar in the annals of American yacht design, stated, ". . . I would say in the first place that these are much better boats than any built since." That is high praise from someone who really knew.

I have no personal memory of the Fish Boat of Dad's because he had sold her a year after my birth, but I did grow up hearing him talk of all the fun that he, Mother, and others had had with her, how she was the best boat he ever owned, and that he wished he never had sold her. Dad had named the boat *West Wind*, the fair wind of lovely summer Maine days. Dianna's and my Scandinavian-designed and -built cruising sloop, a Finngulf 391, bears that same name in homage both to the family legend of a great boat in the past and to memories of my childhood pleasure at peeking out my window overlooking Eggemoggin Reach on awakening in the morning and seeing the boats on their moorings pointing west, usually a sign of a nice day ahead. I was certainly eager to hear what Alec wanted to tell me.

Alec reported that the Fish Boat was still in a condition that could be restored and that a pediatrician in New York was interested in partially funding restoration and having the boat go to the Herreshoff Museum in Bristol, Rhode Island. Would I, Alec wanted to know, consider participating in funding the restoration? My reaction in 2009 was fascination but recognition of other much higher priorities for use of available money—and, I thought then, if I ever restore a boat, it will be to use and enjoy her, not donate her to a museum.

A fine old wooden boat is more than just a boat; it also represents people, heritage, and stories. On that original call from Alec he told me that the provenance of this particular Fish Boat was the most complete of any of the approximately forty Fish Boats built by Herreshoff, that there was more known history about this boat than the others. That in itself gave this particular boat unusual significance. The first twenty-three Fish Boats were designed and built in 1916 for racing by members of the Seawanhaka Corinthian Yacht Club in Oyster Bay, New York, on Long Island Sound. Beginning in the late nineteenth century that yacht club had been an international leader in the development of amateur sailboat racing. There could not have been a more distinguished home in America for the original Fish Boats.

West Wind, originally raced under the name *Sculpin*, was the last of the boats delivered in 1916. The first owner was Franklin Remington, grandson of the inventor of the Remington rifle. The boat remained at Seawanhaka until 1926, when she was sold to an owner in Mattapoisett, Massachusetts, who converted her to marconi rig from the original gaff rig. Fortunately, she escaped the 1938 hurricane, which destroyed the several Fish Boats remaining at Mattapoisett, for in 1932 John Foster Dulles, later Secretary of State under President Eisenhower, bought her and took her back to Oyster Bay until he sold her to Dad in 1937.

Dad briefly kept his Fish Boat near his in-laws' and my grandparents' home across Long Island Sound in Connecticut, but hating Long Island Sound's summer heat and frequent windless days he soon moved her to Brooklin, Maine, where he managed a few weeks of vacation each year until World War II. Very few family photographs of the boat have survived, but they do confirm her being in use on Eggemoggin Reach by 1939. The family does not now know where in Brooklin she sat out all the war years, perhaps in the family boathouse still in use at the edge of Center Harbor. Given memories shared by my older sisters, I take for a certainty that Dad returned her to use after World War II, probably both in 1945 and 1946. He sold her in the fall of the latter year. She went back to Connecticut, even passing through the ownership of Mystic Seaport, the great maritime history museum, during the 1960s, and stayed in that state and under the name *West Wind* through various ownerships and deterioration of her condition as the years passed. She was still there when Alec called me in 2009, derelict with fate uncertain—restoration or chainsaw.

All I could do for Alec after that first call was send him copies of two or three photos that I had discovered following cleaning out my parents' house after their deaths. I more or less put Dad's old Fish Boat out of my mind except for noticing occasionally in the newsletter of Alec's Artisan Boatworks that he continued to look for someone to restore her. Apparently, the pediatrician in New York had not found the inclination or the means to proceed.

In the winter of 2013 Alec's newsletter again mentioned the boat. Curiosity got the better of me. Perhaps dangerously opening myself to temptation, I inquired what had happened over the past four years. The boat was now in Alec's possession at Alec's shop in Rockport, I learned, and with her only an hour and a half away I was dying to see what Dad had always called his favorite boat. Alec preferred to call her by her original name, *Sculpin*, being a believer in the rewards of maintaining originality in historic boats as much as practicality and customers allow. All the original Fish Boats had very appropriately been named after fish species. I was happy to accede to Alec's preference and refer to his derelict as *Sculpin* despite Dad's parenthetical comment "not a very attractive fish" in an old letter that surfaced.

My first visit to Artisan Boatworks was absolutely eye-popping. In the spring before launching time Alec's sheds are full of the most gorgeous sailboats, mostly daysailing size, that one can imagine. Many are either Herreshoff originals or Herreshoff reproductions because Alec has made a particular specialty of them. I followed him through his fleet of cradled boats in complete awe. The cosmetic condition of most of them was flawless—painted topsides smooth and shining and on-deck varnish gleaming, condition so good that it might impair my own enjoyment of actually using such a boat and causing the inevitable dings and scratches.

Then we came to *Sculpin*. I was barely prepared for what I saw. Most paint was gone from her ancient planks, and a few planks were missing, allowing a complete view into the hull interior. The deck had been removed, although a deckhouse, not the original, remained. What I saw was a hulk beyond hope. Alec viewed her optimistically, saying it was a great advantage that the boat had been disassembled to the degree she was. That would have to be done anyway in a restoration, and it was now possible to see clearly what needed to be done. Reusable, he said, were most of the planking, the deadwood (the wood portion of the keel), the lead ballast, most of the metal fittings, and the spars. The boat would need all new frames, a new deck, keelbolts, chainplates, and rudder. He estimated the cost of restoration at 80 percent or less of the cost of building a replica, one of which he had recently completed. What this boat would have, he believed, was its history and soul—and for me, he hoped, a return to being a treasured part of family heritage.

All of this left me with questions. Is a boat resulting from such an extensive restoration the same boat—or is it simply a new boat with many recycled parts? Are we playing mind games with ourselves when we tell ourselves that it would be the same boat? There is no absolute truth as an answer. One can view a restored boat as one wishes. Emotionally, I realized that *Sculpin* did tug upon me. Would I commission a replica? No, for the cost is too high. Would I want another original Fish Boat in good condition if the price were not too steep? Perhaps, because Dad so liked his. Would I like to have Dad's old Fish Boat back on a mooring in Center Harbor? Yes. The emotion coming from all the history and family tradition is real.

Sculpin is indeed art. I took photographs of her in Alec's shed. When I showed one to my son Thor, I heard him murmur, "What a beautiful bow!" The Herreshoff shapes deeply reward the senses, and I often gazed admiringly at that Fish Boat bow in my photograph even as I left commissioning restoration to a future prospect, who indeed materialized eventually. Totally unexpectedly, serendipity would crack the self-discipline that kept me away from Herreshoff Fish Boats. More on that later.

14

THE REWARDS OF BROOKLIN-BUILT SMALL CRAFT

"Welcome to Brooklin—Boatbuilding Capital of the World." Just up the driveway from that sign on the side of Route 175 the late Jim Steele made himself famous in the world of traditional boats by building wooden rowboats to an outstandingly seaworthy and pretty peapod design, which, like the vegetable, is pointed at both ends. His 13-foot-long boats are so captivating in shape that Jim reportedly was flagged down on the Connecticut Thruway with one on top of his truck, and the boat sold right there by the side of the highway.

The original peapods were developed in Maine for lobstering from a rowboat. With their sterns pointed like their bows they maneuvered well forwards and backwards, important when hauling traps in close proximity to dangerous rocks and ledges. We had been lucky enough to have one of these heirlooms in the family, for Dad had had Jim Steele build him one in 1969. When Dianna and I sought a new rowboat for our cruising sailboat, we kept our eyes open for another Jim Steele peapod and found a used one right in our harbor. Jim used to say that he offered three versions: the Chevy with all paint; the Cadillac (which ours is) with varnished sheerstrake (the top plank), rails, and seats; and the Rolls Royce, of which even more is varnished. I find the painting and varnishing an enjoyable rite of spring and a manageable amount of labor. Admiring the results of that labor all summer long is my reward. Dark green topsides with the varnished mahogany sheerstrake make for fun elegance.

More important and fun than the elegance, though, is the actual rowing. Rowing has been important to me since I learned as a tiny boy. In school and college I rowed competitively in four- and eight-oared shells. I even rowed in one more race after college, a highly unusual one. It was against the Somali Navy in the harbor of Chismaio, Somalia, in four-oared Russian lifeboats off a Somalian gunboat! Our destroyer's goodwill visit was long before Somalia descended into its hell of utter chaos. I row for pleasure and for exercise, and Dianna sometimes joins me to row together as a pair. We eschew the noise, dirt, and smell of an outboard. We explore by oar and get back and forth to our cruising boat or to nearby islands by oar in solid, substantial—and lovely—rowboats.

In our peapod we have had innumerable adventures, explored many parts of the coast, and landed on many an island. With the peapod we have accessed, usually many times, some of the finest conserved lands on the coast—the Isle au Haut District of Acadia National Park, Maine Coast Heritage Trust's Marshall Island, the Perry Creek trails of the Vinalhaven Land Trust, Petit Manan National Wildlife Refuge in Steuben, the Passamaquoddy Tribal lands at the wonderfully named Moose Snare Cove, and the less wonderfully named Mud Hole shoreline of The Nature Conservancy at Great Wass Island, to mention a few.

The Mud Hole gave us one of our greatest peapod challenges. Dianna and I took off on a hike on The Nature Conservancy's trails in early to mid-afternoon and for some reason returned considerably later than we planned about an hour before dark. We are well familiar with the 12- to 15- foot rise and fall of tide along the downeast Maine coastline, but we certainly were not paying adequate attention to time or tide that afternoon. A sloping, seaweed-covered ledge over which we had left the peapod floating while tied to a tree was now close to 6 feet out of water. Our biggest problem was that the ledge ended in a vertical drop over which hung the entire back half of our peapod. We could not risk serious damage by simply pushing the boat over this cliff and hoping for the best. Her floating again was hours away, long after dark, and the mosquitoes were already descending. Here literally and figuratively was a real head-scratcher. After some pondering about what to do, we foraged from the woods enough fallen small trees and branches to lay over rocks to cushion the peapod's bottom as we hauled it further up until we reached a point where we could lay down more trees and slide the boat at an angle back toward the water and around the cliff. We stripped off our sweaters and used them to pad especially problematic rocks. With a great deal of pulling and hauling of the heavy boat, our sweaters stained with bottom paint, and our backs still intact we finally relaunched just as dark descended. Adventures like that leave their scars on the peapod. Fortunately, each year's paint and varnish hide most of them.

Exploring by oar has been a particularly educational way to see parts of the Maine coast. The Englishman River lies just east of the famous cruising destination of Roque Island, emptying into Englishman Bay below the long, south-facing beach at Roque Bluffs State Park. On a beautifully clear, early September day we left our cruising sloop *West Wind* anchored in the lee of that beach and with the current giving us a fast ride, rowed under the road bridge into the estuary of the Englishman River. At the time Quoddy Regional Land Trust was pursuing a possible land conservation project not far into the river, and I was eager to see this landscape of low salt marsh with higher forestland behind.

It was migration season. Enthralling was the sheer number of plovers and sandpipers along the winding channel as well as herons, ducks, and other birds that one would expect in such an area. It was an education in how important are these estuarine stopover places along the eastern Maine coast. In my years on the Land for Maine's Future Board I have reviewed many proposals from the Pleasant River Wildlife Foundation requesting funds for the Heads of the Estuaries Project, a partnership that also includes the Maine Department of Inland Fisheries and Wildlife, Maine Coast Heritage Trust, and Downeast Coastal Conservancy. From my rowing and sailing I usually have some familiarity with the areas in which these projects lie, and I always recall that gorgeous afternoon of our peapod exploration into the Englishman River and the proof it provided of the vital role that Maine estuaries play in the lives of migrating birds.

This peapod, so integral to our exploration of the coast, nearly met her end. Earlier in her life she had been caught between a boat and a dock and significantly damaged. She was repaired, but after we bought her, we found that she leaked a bit when towed even though usually not when sitting on a mooring. Pumping after towing was routine. At one point Jim Steele added some stiffening partial frames, which helped, but as years of use passed, I wondered how long she would last given some broken frames and some planks edging out from the abutting ones. Jim said to me more than once, "This boat is good for nothing but burning, Ben." I would always reply, "Jim, why would we want to burn her? We have so much fun with her."

I did say to Dianna, though, that our peapod was one possession that might not outlast us. These worries eventually proved well-founded when, towing the boat up Frenchman Bay alone in late August 2013, I beat into a strong northeast wind and serious chop. Off Ironbound Island she filled to the gunwales. A seam between planks had opened. Heaving to, I brought the peapod near *West Wind*'s stern and fished out the oars and other gear before they floated away. I did not know whether I could tow such a heavy drag the few miles to home, but I also could not just abandon a nearly submerged hazard to navigation. She was easier to tow than I anticipated. Soon enough I had her above the high-tide line on our beach to await her fate—a rebuild or, finally, the burning. With Jim Steele by then deceased, Brooklin boatbuilder Eric Dow fortunately agreed to tackle reframing and refastening. Wooden boats can be rebuilt if not too far gone, and this treasured one probably is now set to outlast us.

❧

Rowing can be an outstanding way to introduce children to the joys of the outdoors and the marine world. How magical that can be was encapsulated for me one sunny summer morning in Center Harbor overseeing adventures of two young grandsons in a wonderful small rowboat. The boys began crabbing with handlines baited with bacon while standing in a stable, lovely wooden dinghy only 8 feet long built at Frank Day's boatyard on Brooklin's Benjamin River in 1952. I accompanied my father to the boatyard the day that he bought her, and over sixty years later here were his great-grandsons enjoying the same boat in the same harbor that was so much home to him.

Soon the boys uncleated themselves from the float, and the oldest, beginning to be competent with oars, rowed inshore to where thick patches of rockweed stood tall in the water and covered the surface. I watched from a distance as they hauled in an occasional crab. After a while the oldest pulled the boat alongside a granite piling of the dock and clambered up the granite blocks to secure the dinghy's painter so that the boat stayed in one place. More crabbing and looking under the rockweed followed before they eventually untied and headed off across the harbor toward Chatto Island. I continued to keep my distance in another rowboat and said almost nothing, letting them pursue their own adventures as they wished.

In a cove in the middle of the island's shoreline they came up with a game of trying to get the dinghy as close to shore as possible without touching bottom, interrupted by the ball cap of the youngest falling in the water and getting stuck under the dinghy. Maneuvering the dinghy to get the cap to float out from underneath posed a significant challenge for a few minutes of much work with the oars and peering over the side. Friction and the pressure of the water kept the cap firmly hidden beneath the boat's bottom. With the soaked, dripping cap eventually back on its owner's head, they headed up the harbor to the gravel beach at the island's eastern end. There they landed, and I watched as they looked for the kinds of treasures that beaches can yield to intrigued youngsters. Satisfied with their beach exploration they climbed back into the little dinghy and stroked strongly back across the harbor to the dock. The oldest had clearly, in that one morning and with no instruction from me, gone from being a beginning rower to a competent one with the quiet pride and self-confidence that mastering such a skill engenders.

That little Frank Day-built dinghy, sized just right for small adventurers, had provided the means for the two boys to explore the joys, lessons, and rewards that the waters and islands of Maine offer. Do such mornings out-of-doors awaken a permanent appreciation for both nature and outdoor activity and a lifelong commitment to the extremely complex task of protecting the environment of this planet that is their home? I can only hope so.

If life only permitted me one boat to use for the exquisite pleasure of enjoying home waters and soaking in the beauty of them, it would be *My Ocean*, a highlight of my life. She is the original Catspaw Dinghy, a rowing, sailing boat built to a Nathanael Herreshoff design slightly modified by Joel White and constructed by Joel at his Brooklin Boat Yard in 1978. There is a school of thought that the enjoyment a vessel gives her owner varies inversely with her size—the smaller the craft, the greater the pleasure. Certainly, small craft are quicker to use and put away, have fewer aggravations, cost far less money, and, importantly to me, place one closer to the water and nature.

In 1977 I wanted to acquire a good rowing boat that also had a rudder, centerboard, and quickly stepped mast. She should be fun to row for pleasure, useful for teaching sailing fundamentals to my then-young children, and good for family picnics to nearby islands. I was eager for my children to know the delight of a quality wooden boat, and I looked forward to the pride of ownership. Having been around Brooklin Boat Yard ever since a young child, I knew that Joel White, a boatbuilder, designer, and expert in traditional watercraft, was the obvious person to whom to turn regarding a boat to suit my needs. On a chilly fall day we stood at his drafting table and discussed possible designs that might work. Joel promised to do more thinking about possibilities.

By total chance—one of those coincidences of life—Dad, who did not know that I wanted such a boat, soon thereafter mailed me a *National Fisherman* clipping which reviewed Mystic Seaport's just published monograph entitled *Building the Herreshoff Dinghy, the Manufacturer's Method*. What immediately caught my eye was the newspaper photograph of a beautiful rowboat under sail with the caption, "The Herreshoff Dinghy sails as well as she rows. The pretty tender is as capable as she looks."

I ordered a copy of the monograph immediately. In the winter of 1975–76 Mystic Seaport had built a replica of an 11½-foot Herreshoff dinghy. The original had been built in 1905 as a lifeboat for the Cup Defender *Columbia*. I was enthralled by the boat described in the monograph and headed off to see Joel again.

Joel agreed that this Herreshoff design would be most suitable. That decided, we discussed minor modifications. The lines would remain unchanged, but my boat would be expanded 10 percent to give more load-carrying capability, making her 12 feet 8 inches long. Instead of lapstrake construction, in which the edges of the planks overlap, my boat would be smooth-planked to provide better abrasion resistance on Maine's rocky beaches. The daggerboard would be replaced by a pivoting centerboard that would pop up should it strike bottom, and the sail with a boom would be replaced by a spritsail. That would get rid of a low, head-crunching boom and enable the spars—mast and sprit—to be short enough to stow within the boat.

Clearly, *My Ocean* was going to be a marvelous small boat, and her building attracted interest. *WoodenBoat* prepared to do a series on her construction. The magazine had always wanted to publish how-to-build articles on unique and practical wooden boats. Following *My Ocean*'s completion, the magazine ordered from Brooklin Boat Yard a sistership so that every step of the building process could be photographed. *WoodenBoat* published a three-part series with the lines and table of offsets accompanied by photographs, drawings, and text detailing the construction. The series was introduced by a beautifully written short piece by Joel and a photograph of him sailing *My Ocean* on builder's trials. Later the series was transformed into the booklet *How to Build the Catspaw Dinghy—a Boat for Oar and Sail.* Somewhere along the way the magazine staff came up with the name Catspaw for this Herreshoff design as modified by Joel.

In use *My Ocean* has been a joy. The spritsail is quick and easy to rig, and the boat is great fun to sail. My pleasure in *My Ocean*'s sailing simplicity as a change from larger, more complex boats has not diminished in the slightest over the years. She is wonderful for sailing explorations into shallow coves and ledge-studded areas, and I do not hesitate to sail her in relatively stiff winds—sitting on the rail and letting the sail luff when necessary.

Sometimes we tow *My Ocean* when cruising. Years ago with children along she provided diversion when at anchor, and she makes a handy and fun way to go after mackerel for breakfast. Although big and heavy by modern standards for a yacht tender, she tows beautifully.

Despite all the other fun, I derive the greatest pleasure from long rows in her. The finest way to start a summer day is to take off before any breeze ruffles the water. In such conditions a boat with clean lines like *My Ocean* will run a long way between strokes. One feels as if one could row forever. For me there is no more enjoyable, healthy, and stress-relieving way to get exercise than to row *My Ocean*. Like our peapod she is a vessel that has provided innumerable exhilarating oar-powered explorations of shorelines and estuaries with endless enjoyment of wildlife and scenic beauty.

My Ocean is a classic, a work of art both in shape and construction, an inspiration to enjoy our coast every day possible, and a storehouse of treasured memories. She more than any boat connects me to the coastal landscape that I call home, and she enshrines wonderful memories of each of my three children.

Thor unwittingly named her at age two-and-a-half. An hour or so after her original launching he stood pointing to her as she lay on a mooring. "My Ocean, My Ocean," he kept saying. We quickly realized that in his vocabulary Thor did not distinguish between the words "boat" and "ocean." To him they meant the same. We had not yet chosen a name for the new vessel, and instantly we realized that that should be it—*My Ocean*.

In the boat's first summer Kristin, age six, began sailing alone while I stood on the float calling instructions. One comical afternoon Kristin's charming great-uncle, an elderly retired physician well into his eighties who was an avid sailor, came down on the float to watch the spectacle, became thoroughly intrigued, and on his own began bellowing orders contradicting mine to the bewildered six-year-old. In a long-kept photograph in my study Chafee is shown a few years later, also at age six, grinning and long hair blowing as she steers *My Ocean* in a race for all sorts of sailboats off Brooklin.

What more can one ask of a boat for Maine? Or of a coastline along which to enjoy her?

15

WASHINGTON COUNTY

Washington County is the nation's easternmost county and the first place in the continental United States to see the rising sun. Over many years it has linked my passions for being afloat on salt water and conserving Maine's stunning coastal environment, all the while engaging me with the local culture that this land-and-seascape nourishes. In the twenty-first century Washington County's people struggle with limited economic opportunities and a declining, aging population. Lobstering, lucrative at least for now, holds sway in the coastal towns, and vast acreages are devoted to working forests.

Washington County has some of Maine's finest and least-developed lakes and most of the remaining salmon rivers. The coastline is markedly different from the coast farther west. Long, wooded peninsulas extend far out, separated by bays with delightful coves, islands, and salt marshes. At Cutler the so-called Bold Coast begins, a long, relatively straight and rugged shoreline of mostly cliffs bordering Grand Manan Channel and ending at West Quoddy Head, the easternmost point in the continental United States. The Washington County coastline entranced me on my first sailing cruise along it at age fourteen. It still entrances—and very much inspires me—today.

Dianna and I usually leave in late August for a week or more sailing along the Washington County coast. The first day of the cruise, rounding Acadia National Park's Schoodic Point and steering past Petit Manan lighthouse eight miles farther east, is a high point of the year. *A Cruising Guide to the New England Coast*, for decades the information bible for people cruising New England, wonderfully captures the excitement:

> *To be headed east by Schoodic bell before a summer sou'wester with Mt. Desert fading astern and the lonely spike of Petit Manan Light just visible on the port bow is about as close to perfection as a man*

can expect to come on this imperfect earth.

For the experienced navigator with a touch of the explorer, this country is the Promised Land . . .

Changing attitudes in our society may explain why the first sentence of the above passage differs amusingly from the introductory sentence of the same section of earlier editions of *A Cruising Guide to the New England Coast*. Wrote the authors in the earlier editions:

It is an old tradition among cruising men that all hands receive an extra round of grog on passing Schoodic Point bound east.

When we round Schoodic, we skip the grog, but I smile at that old passage in the cruising guide and miss those grog imbibers, who so loved to sail this coast and many of whom worked very hard to conserve its scenic and natural qualities.

I was privileged to enjoy a magnificent introduction to the region. On a spectacularly clear day in mid-August of 1959, Dad, my cousin Jack, and I cast off the Center Harbor mooring of Dad's husky wooden sloop *Arcturus*, hoisted sail in a morning northwester following passage of a cold front, and bore off for eastern Maine. This would be our first sailing cruise way downeast to Washington County. We treasured our tricks at the wheel as *Arcturus* romped along before a fresh wind that gradually swung to the southwest—a perfect day for heading east. No grog was served as we passed Schoodic Point, but Dad had me hand up from the galley a Heineken beer for him and peanut butter and strawberry jam sandwiches.

Late afternoon, well to the east of Petit Manan Light, brought us abeam of the outer shore of Great Wass Island and then rapidly to the entrance to the intriguingly named Cow Yard at Head Harbor Island. The strong afternoon wind was humping up a bit of a sea, and waves crashed on the sloping granite on both sides of the entrance, Steele Harbor Island's shore to port and small Man Island to starboard. We scudded between them into the Cow Yard. I let go the anchor, and here we were, anchored in a Washington County cove for the first time.

Most fortunately for me, there would be many more such anchorings in the years ahead, but I still cannot pass the Cow Yard without thinking of that exciting, beautiful first arrival.

The memory of my first arrival was also very much in my mind about fifteen years later when on behalf of Maine Coast Heritage Trust I worked with the owners of Head Harbor Island and Steele Harbor Island on conservation easements for those islands. My knowledge of the islands gained from sailing cruises to the area was very helpful both in establishing credibility with the islands' owners and with being able to provide sound advice related to crafting the conservation easements. All development was prohibited on Steele Harbor Island, and the conservation easement over most of Head Harbor Island very severely restricted development beyond the existing small house and dock overlooking the Cow Yard. These conservation easements were granted to the National Audubon Society and later transferred to The Nature Conservancy after National Audubon decided that it preferred not to have responsibility for conservation easements far afield from its Hog Island facility in Muscongus Bay, well to the westward. One of the owning couple, Priscilla Williams, joined the board of directors of Maine Coast Heritage Trust and was active on the board and, indeed, treasurer for a number of years. She and her husband Doug were marvelously generous, like so many other island owners, to preserve the scenic and natural qualities of their lovely islands for the benefit of all who cherish the Maine coast.

Just a few miles away Dianna and I recently enjoyed a heartwarming experience that speaks volumes about people who make their lives in the region year-round. In a cove on the west side of Roque Island we were preparing to anchor just before sunset one Sunday when we realized that an overtaking lobsterboat was slowing with the clear intention of conversing. As his boat, the *Nancy Anne,* idled alongside, the fisherman called over, "It's lobsterman's Halloween trick-or-treat. Want some lobsters? There's no charge." We were delighted at the prospect of a lobster dinner but stressed that we certainly wanted to pay him. "No, no," he countered, and, motioning to his wife and two young boys on board, continued, "We are teaching the boys about gifting.

These Are lobsters that they caught. Hand over a bucket." Over went
the bucket, and with the parents smiling and the boys looking dubious
and probably less than thrilled, back came dinner. Nearly two months
later when real Halloween arrived, Dianna tracked down the school
secretary at the boys' elementary school. Dianna sent a Halloween card
with a donation for the school and immediately received back a big
card of thanks signed by every child and with notes from the boys who
had given us their lobsters.

(We once had a far different experience with a lobsterboat coming
near, this one in Eggemoggin Reach. I was in the cabin, and Dianna at
the wheel was the only person visible on deck. Up from astern came a
fisherman to pass close alongside. As he came next to us, he held toward
Dianna a large hand-made sign with large letters shouting, "Show me
your tits!")

Like the lobsterman on the *Nancy Anne*, another local resident had
equally surprised and delighted me some years earlier. A bird nesting
island in the Roque archipelago is Halifax Island, once mostly devoid
of trees but now growing back and lying at the eastern end of the string
of islands south of the Great Beach. Halifax Island is the only island
in the Roque archipelago under a different ownership. When I was
representing The Conservation Fund in Maine in the early 1990s and
my colleague, Ken Olson, later longtime president of Friends of Acadia,
was working for the Fund out of its Arlington, Virginia, headquarters,
Ken arranged for The Conservation Fund to purchase Halifax Island
for resale to the U.S. Fish and Wildlife Service.

Ken was concerned about how the municipal officials in Jonesport
would react to the news that the island, which lies within the town's
boundaries, was going to be federal property. He asked me to meet
with the selectmen. I arranged a meeting with them and drove down
to Jonesport unsure of what reception I would receive when I gave the
selectmen the news. I was most surprised—and relieved—when great
enthusiasm was expressed. It turned out that the cove on the western
end of Halifax Island was the favorite duck hunting spot for one of the
selectmen. Hunting would be permitted, and the selectman was ecstatic
that the cove would stay as it was.

Some distance east from Halifax Island lies the far-downeast community of Cutler. Numerous times we have anchored in its well-protected harbor, and it has been the site of some fascinating conservation challenges. Maine Coast Heritage Trust was fortunate to have for many years an energetic member of its board of directors from Cutler—Jasper Cates, a burly fisherman and community leader who was a wonderfully appealing man. I never tired of his colorful way of not mincing words. Said he about a mutual acquaintance, "He's so crooked that when he dies, they're going to screw him into the ground."

Daily on his way out of the harbor to tend his lobster traps Jasper passed under the dramatic cliffs of Western Head. By 1989 this spectacular rugged headland was in foreclosure following failure of a development scheme. Jasper strongly encouraged Maine Coast Heritage Trust to try to preserve Western Head in its wild state. The organization's then-president Jay Espy asked me to go to the foreclosure auction and try to buy the headland for Maine Coast Heritage Trust.

On a dreary, raw, mid-December Saturday, Bar Harbor attorney Doug Chapman and I drove to Cutler for the auction. To keep Maine Coast Heritage Trust's profile as low as possible, Doug would not actually attend the auction but would wait in Jasper's brother's kitchen in the village in case I succeeded in placing a winning bid and papers needed to be reviewed and signed. Doug never went anywhere on business except in a suit and tie, and I made the mistake of asking him what I should wear. Suit and tie, he answered. I took Doug's advice, but when I joined the group receiving homemade donuts as we waited to go into the rural farmhouse where the auction was to be held, I felt ridiculous in my citified gray suit. My principal competitor for the property, a real estate developer, arrived in a white knit shirt with gold chains around his neck. In this fishing community we probably both looked as if we had dropped in from other, although separate, planets, but at least, unlike him, I was not driving a white Cadillac with gold trim and New York license plates. As it turned out, the minimums set by the bank were too high for any prospective bidders. Western Head did not sell that day, but over a prolonged period of subsequent months, Jay was finally able to procure Western Head as a Maine Coast Heritage Trust preserve.

Just northeast of Halifax Island, where the Jonesport selectman loved to shoot ducks, one can enter Little Kennebec Bay, which in shape seems more a river than a bay. In a southwest wind it is a lovely run under sail up Little Kennebec Bay and through the increasingly narrow channel in its Collins Branch until one reaches the end at Moose Snare Cove. One can only wonder how that name came to be. Although we can fit our sailboat into the cove's tight confines, because of all the lobster buoys in the cove we always choose to anchor just outside on the south side of a small wooded island.

The west shore of the long finger of water that is the Collins Branch is Johnson Point. When we first landed on Johnson Point, it already had a gravel road almost to the end and was staked out as a subdivision that was being advertised in local newspapers. The road led north to lovely, rolling blueberry land overlooking Moose Snare Cove and the Collins Branch. The owner, the Passamaquoddy Tribe, was abandoning active management of the land for blueberries. In the early years of visiting in late summer we had marvelous berry-picking, but it has deteriorated as brushy vegetation has taken over the formerly managed land. One of our pleasures over the years from stopping and hiking at Moose Snare Cove has been watching Maine Coast Heritage Trust succeed in preserving Johnson Point by buying it and then, in a very creative project, receive a conservation easement over the abutting Passamaquoddy land in return for helping the Tribe acquire a parcel of great cultural significance to the Tribe farther east.

One year approaching Moose Snare Cove, we were astonished to see ahead on the Passamaquoddy property a number of small, rustic buildings. We landed for our usual hike, that day leaving our peapod on the shore below the buildings, which appeared to be some sort of instant village. We saw no one as we passed by. A couple of hours later returning from our hike we encountered a small group of people, who even at a distance we could see were oddly dressed. They seemed eager to see us and chat. We learned that they were actors in a film on colonial

America being prepared for public television. Suddenly, up strode a hostile woman who belligerently confronted us about what we were doing on the land. We told her that we had hiked there for years. With difficulty we persuaded her that we were going to have to continue across the land and pass by the village again to reach our peapod. She absolutely forbade us to talk any more with the actors. They grinned at us in amusement. It turned out that in order to have the movie as realistic as possible, the actors were being isolated from the world outside their village and were surrounded by security people, who had missed seeing our arrival.

By our next visit the village was completely gone. Perhaps television producers have to go all the way to eastern Maine to find land on salt water sufficiently unspoiled for such a film about New England life in the 1600s.

Every summer's cruise to eastern Maine has kept my interest in Washington County very much alive, but for some years after the mid-1990s I did not have much role in the increasing pace of conservation efforts along that part of the Maine coast. Then in 2009 I received a telephone call from Les Coleman in Addison asking whether I would serve on the board of the Downeast Coastal Conservancy, the new entity resulting from the merger of Great Auk Land Trust and Quoddy Regional Land Trust. Les had been the dynamic chair of the Great Auk board and would be chairing Downeast Coastal Conservancy.

By then I had been appointed by Governor Baldacci to the Land for Maine's Future Board and was off all other land conservation boards. To avoid conflicts of interest and the need to recuse myself from Land for Maine's Future votes because of such conflicts, I had intended to stay off the board of any organization that might apply to the Land for Maine's Future Program for project funding. In the case of Downeast Coastal Conservancy, however, I decided to break that self-imposed rule.

The merging of the two smaller land trusts into the new Downeast

Coastal Conservancy was a major step forward for land conservation in eastern Maine. This merger was challenging because of the two very different cultures and histories of Quoddy Regional Land Trust and Great Auk Land Trust. Merging was reportedly almost voted down by one of the two boards. The new board of directors was composed of people who had been on the pre-merger boards with two exceptions—me and one other. Given my joy from our annual sailing cruises along the Washington County coast and the treasured memories of the rewarding land conservation projects in which I had been involved there, especially Great Auk Land Trust's acquisition of Browney Island, now a Downeast Coastal Conservancy preserve, I found most appealing the opportunity to reengage in land conservation east of Schoodic. I hoped that my experience over forty years might be helpful in getting Downeast Coastal Conservancy off to a strong start. I also knew that this still small eastern Maine land trust was blessed with some exceptionally able and dedicated people, including Tom Boutureira, its talented young executive director at the time, and had strong support from both The Nature Conservancy and Maine Coast Heritage Trust.

My four years on the Downeast Coastal Conservancy board included the remarkable Two Rivers Project, which is an important model for the nation. As I said about it as keynote speaker at the land trust's annual meeting in 2013, "This is land conservation at its best. It does good for the land, and it does good for the people." With the Two Rivers Project the Downeast Coastal Conservancy purchased two parcels of land totaling over 1,000 acres and four-and-a-half miles of riverfront. Over 100 acres of that is on the Middle River on the east side of downtown Machias. Its fields and woods have long been enjoyed by residents. At the other end of town and stretching into Whitneyville are over 900 acres of well-stocked woodlands on the Machias River.

The two parcels are connected by the Sunrise Trail, the former railroad line that has been converted to a recreational trail for foot traffic, biking, and ATVs and snowmobiles. Machias is the county seat for Washington County and home to the University of Maine at Machias. Like all of Washington County it seeks economic stimulation. Never have I seen a land conservation project that so links land conservation to economic benefits and to recreation, education, and wellness also. These two parcels, linked by the Sunrise Trail, which passes close to the local schools and hospital, have the potential to attract more visitors to Machias who seek to take advantage of the recreational opportunities on the land and improved access to the rivers for fishing and paddling. The properties offer opportunities for nature education and connecting youth to the outdoors, provide an attractive setting for outdoor physical exercise, and can be a community forest able to heighten local understanding of forest management for tree health and wildlife habitat. The multiple benefits of the Two Rivers Project are well captured by the overarching phrase used during the campaign for the necessary funds: "Community Revitalization Through Conservation."

Much local enthusiasm was generated. A large local committee formed to promote the project, members of which came from a pleasingly wide swath of community interests. There is now much more focus on engaging local communities in land conservation than there was years ago. We used to think that protecting scenic and natural qualities of land was sufficient without as much direct engagement of local people or as much focus on providing public access and opportunities for recreation and outdoor education. The Two Rivers Project is a very twenty-first-century project that captures the emphasis on community engagement, and because of that attracted strong support from funders. It is indeed an important model for the land conservation world.

Trips back and forth to Washington County by boat and by car for sheer fun on the water or for land conservation endeavors have all been enjoyable, rewarding, and hugely inspiring. As we head west at the end of each cruise and pass the demarcation point of Petit Manan, I always look forward to the next time our bow points eastward. We have had some grand sails home over the years, though—sometimes an invigoratingly hard beat into the prevailing summer southwest winds or a close reach in September's brisk northwesters. On other days we have powered westward in flat calms, frequently accompanied by thick fog and occasionally cold rain. Even when headed west and leaving Washington County astern, sailing along this coastline can be, to quote the cruising guide again, "about as close to perfection as a man can expect to come on this imperfect earth"!

16

CUTLER CHALLENGES

One land conservation project in Washington County took more of my attention and time than all the others there together. In the 1980s and for many prior years the parcel of mainland on the Maine coast with the longest stretch of privately owned shoreline, about three-and-a-half miles, was the approximately 2,100 acres between Route 191 and Grand Manan Channel just east of Cutler village. It belonged to the Pejepscot Paper Company, a subsidiary of the Hearst Corporation. Wild and of rugged topography, its conservation significance was obvious, but its scale put it beyond the (then) capabilities of Maine Coast Heritage Trust. The Conservation Fund was asked to become engaged; Peggy Rockefeller opened the door to the chairman of Hearst; and because I still had involvement with Maine Coast Heritage Trust in regard to Washington County's Bold Coast, I was asked to accompany The Conservation Fund's president Pat Noonan to a meeting in New York with Hearst's chairman.

Pat is someone whom I had known for years, going back to when he was president of The Nature Conservancy before he founded The Conservation Fund. At one time, Pat had asked whether I might like to be considered to run the Conservancy's Chesapeake Bay program, and we had stayed in touch over the years. With The Conservation Fund he created an organization that originally was focused almost entirely on purchasing lands sought by the U.S. Fish and Wildlife Service, the National Park Service, and state conservation agencies. Because a private, nonprofit organization can often act much more rapidly than a government agency, The Conservation Fund's ability to buy, then resell to government agencies frequently has made the difference between successfully seizing or losing important conservation opportunities.

Pat and I had our fruitful first meeting with the Hearst Corporation's chairman in Manhattan, and later, on a scorching August day, we

hiked the land with Hearst's forester. If there were trails on the parcel
fronting on Grand Manan Channel at that time, I do not remember
them. I do remember hot slogging in the open areas of the rugged ter-
rain of mixed grass and rocky outcroppings. Pat, who spent more time
behind a desk than I did and who had just arrived from his Arlington,
Virginia, office, looked like he might expire. In fact, I became a bit
worried as sweat poured off his increasingly flushed face and he gasped,
"I hadn't realized we were going on a Vietnam-like experience!" We all
survived, though, and Pat went on successfully to carry out purchase
negotiations.

I was not involved with those subsequent purchase negotiations by
The Conservation Fund. By then I had disappeared on another winter
family sailing cruise from Maine to the eastern Caribbean and back. In
order to buy the approximately 2,100 acres on the shore, The Conservation Fund also had to agree to buy 9,000 acres in the same Hearst
ownership directly across Route 191 and stretching north into Whiting. The shorefront parcel was immediately resold to Maine's Department of Conservation. To pay The Conservation Fund, the State used
bond money from the first round of the Land for Maine's Future Program. Trails and campsites were created, and the parcel became known
as the Cutler Coast Public Reserved Lands. At that time the State was
not interested in owning the land north of Route 191. The Richard
King Mellon Foundation provided The Conservation Fund with the
capital to acquire that parcel and hold it while the Fund sought a long-
term conservation solution for the land.

I had returned from our tropic family sailing adventure by the time
The Conservation Fund was beginning serious ownership and management planning for the 9,000 acres it now possessed in Cutler and
Whiting. The Conservation Fund did not wish to be more than an
interim owner, but it had no clear idea of who should own the land for
the long run. The funder, Mellon, had a program priority of funding
purchases of habitat for fish and wildlife, and an important goal was to

find a long-term solution that took the habitat priority into account.

I was asked by The Conservation Fund whether I would be will-ing to represent it with a dual set of tasks. One task was to work with the local community in Cutler and, to a lesser extent, Whiting, where there was far less acreage, to identify who would be the best perma-nent owner. My subsequent seemingly endless meetings with commu-nity leaders and others in these towns probably were one of the earliest examples in Maine of a land conservation organization's deeply engag-ing with a local community in order to try to make long-term decisions that properly protect a property's natural qualities in a way that the community would favor.

My other task for The Conservation Fund would be to identify pre-acquisition opportunities for purchasing lands wanted by the United States Fish and Wildlife Service for its National Wildlife Refuges in Maine and possibly lands wanted by Acadia National Park. If there were opportunities to assist state conservation agencies, that could be part of my job too. By then I was doing some limited consulting work for several conservation efforts, and I was pleased to work on behalf of The Conservation Fund. Knowing that finding the solution for the big Cutler parcel would take time, The Conservation Fund leased it to Maine Coast Heritage Trust so that the Trust could handle the interim land management. Maine Coast Heritage Trust assigned its responsi-bilities to its talented and experienced staff person Caroline Norden, whom I both much respected and enjoyed. I looked forward to the Cutler adventure together.

Indeed, the next several years of close collaboration turned out to be just that—an adventure, very enjoyable, and, in fact, most challeng-ing. The land's conservation significance other than sheer size was not immediately clear and took time to comprehend. A parcel of that size could be expensive to manage. Much of Cutler was already in govern-ment or nonprofit ownership due to the presence of the Navy commu-nications station, Cross Island's having been acquired by the U.S. Fish and Wildlife Service, Western Head's having been acquired by Maine Coast Heritage Trust, and, of course, the shorefront former Hearst parcel's having been bought by the State. Cutler is a tiny community, which had little of an economy other than fishing, woods work, and the Navy. Taking more land off the tax rolls was understandably of great local concern, as was loss of local control.

Adding to the challenges was the fact that eastern coastal Washington County at that time was home to a strident, if small, group of vocal people captivated by the national anti-government property rights movement. The messiah of the property rights movement was Chuck Cushman, who had founded the National In-Holders Association, originally an organization for private owners of properties surrounded by or abutting government-owned properties. They fought further government acquisitions, and they often opposed land acquisition by nonprofit conservation organizations as well. When I began my late 1980s and 1990s work in Washington County for Maine Coast Heritage Trust and The Conservation Fund, I had hoped to take advantage of Chuck Cushman's owing me a favor. At least, I thought he owed me a favor.

Near the end of my time as executive director of the Land Trust Exchange, we had held the second of our National Rallies for land trusts at the extraordinary Asilomar facility owned by the State of California on the Monterey Peninsula. Chuck had gained national publicity—some of us might have said notoriety—for his aggressive anti-government tactics and whipping up hysteria among landowners. Chuck decided to show up at Asilomar. On the first evening he waited outside the dining hall for me to go into dinner, stopped me, and introduced himself. He asked if we might sit together, which we did. He had an agenda, but he was courteous. Rather than risk his being a heckler at presentations planned for the next day, I offered him a chance to speak when all the attendees would be gathered in the main lecture hall. Taken aback by friendly outreach from a conservationist, he looked quite surprised before accepting.

As I passed the word later that evening that Chuck would be speaking the next morning, I found that I had equally surprised the attendees and was being criticized. Some colleagues tried to persuade me that Chuck would hijack the Rally by going off on tirades that would create a ruckus and divert attention from the networking and educational purposes of the event. Those who had not heard about this addition to the agenda were flabbergasted as they sat in the big hall the next morning and heard me announce that I was sticking to my guns and offering Chuck the podium. Up he stood, made clear that he believed that no one from the conservation world had ever treated him decently before, and said that he felt like, in his words, "the skunk at the garden party." He was gracious, brief, and sat down. We now had heard his perspective directly from him. He had done no damage to our Rally and, in fact, had added substance.

It was only three or four years later that I was working on the Bold Coast projects when I read in a newspaper that the property rights group in Washington County was expecting a visit from Chuck Cushman. Perhaps naïve to hope that Chuck might believe that he owed me a favor, I decided to try to head him off. I got him on the phone, but, not surprisingly, my encouragement to him to cancel his Washington County trip went nowhere. He came and stiffened the resolve of those who seemed to think that any permanent conservation of land was bad.

My years working on the big Cutler parcel project were to include a great deal of careful communication with and cultivating a decent relationship with those property rights folks. They formed their own nonprofit, named it the Maine Conservation Rights Institute, and once even invited me to one of their board meetings to discuss the Cutler parcel. For someone from a conservation organization to attend a board meeting of theirs was a first. It was an interesting, delicate relationship—but courteous—which I maintained with them. In the end, the property rights movement's local contingent did not undercut us, but I treated them with kid gloves.

꒰ꑄ

Caroline Norden and I plunged into our Cutler duties with considerable enthusiasm. Prior to joining the Maine Coast Heritage Trust staff, she had graduated from the Yale School of Forestry and run a land trust in Connecticut. Her land management knowledge was excellent, and she was a dogged worker. I found her the perfect colleague for

the Cutler project. With Maine Coast Heritage Trust's having taken
on day-to-day management through its lease from The Conservation
Fund, Caroline's responsibilities included managing local use of natural
resources such as providing permits for harvesting firewood and tipping
for Christmas wreaths. She leased a small area of blueberries to a local
grower. Caroline also was a vital adviser to me and The Conservation
Fund on issues related to long-term ownership and local politics.

As we came to know the land north of Route 191 better, we realized, as so often happens in land conservation, that it had more conservation significance than originally recognized when the focus had
been on the shorefront parcel south of the road. Part of the land was
indeed timberland typical of the area, but a vast part of it was grasslands
such as I have not personally seen elsewhere in Maine. One April day
a group of us traversed these grasslands to gain a better feel for them.
I could not help but compare what I was seeing to some savannah in
Africa, a tiny glimpse of which I had had in a brief game park outing
during a Navy port visit to the Kenyan city of Mombasa. I had no idea
that Maine had such extensive grasslands, and my conservation colleagues were astounded too at what we discovered in Cutler and Whiting. What explained the presence of these grasslands? How long had
they been there? And why had they not grown back into trees? No one
seemed to have clear answers.

Almost certainly fire had been part of the regimen that had maintained the grasslands, perhaps well before European settlement. We
did know for sure that in recent times fires were purposely set by deer
hunters in the spring when the ground was covered with combustible
dead grass in order to keep areas from growing up too much. On the
April day that we set out across the grasslands, we even saw such a fire
burning along a roadside, and we knew to be very, very careful out on
the grasslands at that time of year—to keep an eye peeled to windward
for any sign of smoke. To be caught downwind of a fire in all that grass
could be catastrophic. We did succeed in crossing them that day, jumping the narrow stream that wends its way through the grass.

The presence of that stream was the root cause of my engaging
not long thereafter with one of the more unusual characters—perhaps

sinister, perhaps just pathetic—whom I met during my work in land conservation. At the north end of the property was a 500-acre protrusion into it owned by a New Yorker. This parcel had legal access but was a long way from either Route 1 to the north or Route 191 to the south. It had very little practical utility, but it did have some of the grasslands and significant frontage on the narrow stream. The prior owner had advertised it in *The Wall Street Journal*, emphasizing the many feet of stream frontage. It may well be true that there is a sucker born every minute, and Frank—let that be enough of a name for this aging New Yorker of Italian descent—took the bait. All that Maine waterfront— and to a New Yorker seemingly so cheap—should be a great way to make some easy money by selling waterfront lots.

He bought the land sight unseen, then showed up at the realtor's office for a tour of his new domain. The realtor later told me the story of that tour. Off they bounced down the old woods road that provided access, farther and farther from Route 1. When they finally reached where they could see more than just the dark trees crowding the sides of the rough access road, Frank was too scared to get out of the truck. Frank, who may have spent his days in quite scary company in New York, was terrified that a coyote might get him!

To protect the overall ecological integrity of its holding and to straighten the boundary, The Conservation Fund was eager to purchase Frank's land. I went to New York to discuss a purchase, and we met at a somewhat seedy restaurant north of the city, sitting in a corner where Frank could both see anyone else and have privacy for our chat. Frank was obviously very eager to sell. He told me that a little business of his was under great pressure to make payments on loans. He must have realized that almost no one other than The Conservation Fund would be interested in his remote property that was useless for almost anything other than ecological conservation. As expected, though, Frank professed a conviction that his waterfront property was valuable. He named his price. Then he paused, looked at me, and went straight to what he hoped would be the clincher. If I would get The Conservation Fund to pay his asking price, he would give me a percentage under the table. I was flabbergasted enough to just sit there dumbstruck, wondering whether I had heard him correctly. My lack of reaction completely unnerved him. It was clear that he was afraid that I was about to stand up and stalk out, leaving him without any prospect of a land buyer to provide his much-needed money. "I didn't offend you, did I?" he said with much concern in his voice as he leaned toward me and continued, "You have to understand that is how we do business in New York."

"Well, we don't do that in Maine—or, at least, the people I know don't," I responded. Having put that to rest, I continued the conversation about a purchase, making a mental note to report the bribe offer to Pat Noonan at The Conservation Fund as soon as possible in case Frank should try to frame me as having solicited it. That is the only time in all my years engaged in land conservation that I have ever been offered a bribe.

Frank had no choice except to deal with me on my terms if he wanted to sell. We went through the usual process of commissioning an appraisal and making an offer based on the appraisal, which Frank accepted without too much grumbling. A small, elderly man in a black raincoat who made dumb mistakes and was under who knew what pressures in his New York world, Frank was someone for whom I felt sorry and actually kind of liked.

Finding a permanent owner for all that land of The Conservation Fund turned out to be difficult. On the one hand, the Richard King Mellon Foundation was adamant that the land remain in conservation ownership that could be counted on for the long run, and the Foundation had a strong preference for the U.S. Fish and Wildlife Service. It was willing, however, to entertain other possibilities that Caroline and I might suggest. In Cutler any more federal ownership within the town was a very hard sell. The Conservation Fund, and particularly Maine Coast Heritage Trust, could not afford politically to appear to run rough-shod over local opinion. Doug Mullen, then manager of Moosehorn National Wildlife Refuge, did want to acquire the parcel as an addition to Moosehorn, and he eagerly accepted our invitation to speak at a public meeting in Cutler.

I have never forgotten a comment from the floor that winter evening in the Cutler Library, where we held many meetings with local residents and town officials as we tried to find a solution satisfactory to at least a majority locally that also would meet the criteria of the Mellon Foundation. Doug described the types of visitors that National Wildlife Refuges attract. He talked about how low-impact they are, bringing only cameras, binoculars, and perhaps bicycles. He seemed to imply that visitors to National Wildlife Refuges are a cut above some of the masses that descend on national parks. As soon as Doug finished his talk, an older man from Cutler popped to his feet and, staring directly at Doug, emphatically exclaimed, "In Cutler we don't care whether tourists are good tourists or bad tourists. We don't want tourists!" And with that he sat down.

I had run across antipathy to tourists before, and I am still cautious about it. Twenty years before that Cutler meeting, Acadia National Park had been proposing the acquisition of Marshall Island for wilderness camping. Stonington would be the access point, as it is for Isle au Haut. Stonington in that era feared the prospective increase in visitors and was vocal about it. I never knew whether it was true, but word had it then that Stonington resisted having public restrooms as part of discouraging tourists. Today, with restaurants, art and crafts galleries, and many more people "from away" having settled on Deer Isle, Stonington obviously has a sizable percentage of its population that invites tourists.

As is so often the case in small towns, discomfort with outsiders can run deep. I at times found astounding what people would say in a public meeting. One of the issues on which I worked was the desire on some residents' part to see more land available at affordable prices for young community members who wanted to stay in Cutler and raise families. The Conservation Fund parcel came close to the village's east side and restricted expansion in that direction. The harbor prevented expansion to the west. The Conservation Fund was willing to make some acreage close to the village available for affordable housing, and it even paid for my taking an affordable housing consultant to Cutler to meet with people interested in the idea.

One hurdle that we encountered quickly was that local interest centered on affordable—cheap—land, not houses. Local preference seemed to be to buy a house lot at low cost, then put up whatever one might want as a house. In a place like Cutler a high proportion of residents have the know-how to build a house and have skilled friends and relatives willing to help. Our affordable housing consultant was used to projects where homes were built by an affordable housing developer, then sold at subsidized prices with limits on future sale prices so that prices would remain affordable as time passes. Affordable land as opposed to affordable housing is, he told us, a prescription for a rural slum, something that The Conservation Fund wanted no part of. While some residents encouraged some sort of affordable housing project, others were vehemently against. The opposition of those against was partly fueled by fear that such a project would attract outsiders. An older man stood up at one meeting and said something so racist about the possibility of outsiders being attracted that I am still astonished that at the end of the twentieth century in the United States, especially in Maine, someone would have said what he said in a public meeting even if he thought it.

We spent seven years searching for the best solution to the long-term conservation ownership of The Conservation Fund land. Early on, I approached all the obvious candidates in addition to the U.S. Fish and Wildlife Service—the State of Maine, The Nature Conservancy, and Maine Coast Heritage Trust. Except for the Fish and Wildlife Service, we were finding no takers for the considerable management burden and cost in a politically delicate environment until we talked to the University of Maine Foundation.

The idea of ownership by the Foundation was very well received locally. The University of Maine Foundation viewed the timber on the land, while limited, as sufficient to promise a revenue stream to help support the University's forestry school. The Richard King Mellon Foundation was less enthusiastic about University-connected ownership, having seen too many universities dispose of land possessing conservation values with no effort to protect those values. Caroline and I knew that ownership by the University of Maine Foundation would have to be supplemented by a conservation easement held by the U.S. Fish and Wildlife Service. However, the dean of the forestry school opposed having management of the land restricted in any way by a conservation easement, and the University idea faded.

In the end, the Maine Department of Conservation's Bureau of Public Lands changed its mind and came to the conclusion that it wanted the land and would manage it for multiple uses—recreation, timber management, and ecological preservation. Local support for that solution was good, and the Richard King Mellon Foundation acquiesced, even sweetening the transfer by funding an endowment for ongoing payments in lieu of taxes so that Cutler and Whiting would receive a revenue stream approximately equal to what they would receive under Maine's current use assessment laws. When title was transferred to the state, The Conservation Fund deeded about 200 acres behind the village to Maine Coast Heritage Trust to bank the land for affordable housing in case that concept could proceed in the future.

For a gift of land that the State had originally declined, Maine made a big deal of the donation from the Richard King Mellon Foundation. Governor Angus King asked many of us who had been associated with this lengthy conservation project to come to his office in the state capitol building for a press conference. What we had not realized until we arrived, and which the state loudly trumpeted, was that the gift was the second largest land gift to the state ever—second only to Baxter State Park. It pales in comparison to Baxter, but, nonetheless, the point was striking.

I—and others too, I think—came away from the Cutler project having learned or had reinforced a number of useful lessons. They are worth setting down:

- Skilled land conservation organizations can assemble large amounts of non-governmental dollars to acquire significant large properties;
- government dollars may also be available to assist with a purchase;
- well-known and respected people can help open doors to

landowners;

- acquisition of a large property by a nonprofit conservation organization does not require knowing at the time of acquisition exactly what will be the permanent conservation solution in terms of ownership and management;
- temporary ownership as well as permanent ownership requires planning and careful stewardship;
- additional abutting acquisitions may be needed to protect natural systems;
- conservation organizations can work successfully with local communities to achieve shared conservation, social, and economic goals, including "banking" land for future possible needs; and
- successful solutions will be determined by a combination of local opinions, the owning conservation entity's goals, and, importantly, the wishes of the major funding sources.

I hugely enjoyed the challenges of the Cutler project and felt that I had successfully walked a political tightrope between factions in the local community, some of which were influenced by the area's property rights contingent. I much enjoyed getting to know many of the people of Cutler. During those years, though, a bit to Dianna's frustration, we stopped going there when cruising along the eastern Maine coast. I obviously was an outsider anyway, but, nonetheless, appearing in the fishing harbor in a sailing yacht might affect my relationships in town in ways that I did not dare test. It was years before we again anchored in Little River, that lovely and remote Cutler harbor way downeast.

17

LAND FOR MAINE'S FUTURE—THE BEST AND WORST OF TIMES

The importance to Maine of the Land for Maine's Future Program is well illustrated by the Cutler coastlands project described in the previous chapter. The program funded the State's purchase of the largest privately owned parcel of mainland shorefront, three-and-a-half miles of shore just east of Cutler village. One of the most worthwhile conservation activities in which I have ever engaged and of which I am proudest is serving two terms on the Land for Maine's Future Board.

Governor Baldacci's appointing me to the Land for Maine's Future Board in 2007 was preceded many, many months earlier by a telephone call from Jay Espy, then still president of Maine Coast Heritage Trust. There were vacancies on the Land for Maine's Future Board, and Maine Coast Heritage Trust wanted to suggest some candidates to the Governor's office. Jay asked whether I had any ideas. We chatted about some possibilities before he queried, what about me, would I be interested in serving?

Since its inception in 1987 the Land for Maine's Future Program has established an outstanding track record of wisely using bond dollars approved by the legislature and voters to help fund the conservation of over 600,000 acres of some of Maine's finest lands. These include areas for outdoor recreation, vital wildlife habitat, scenic vistas, access to water bodies, and archaeological sites. The monies have been used too for conservation easement purchases on working forestlands and farms as well as for restrictions to keep working waterfront facilities permanently available for use by the fishing industry. "Yes," I said to Jay, "I'd be honored to be considered for appointment to the Land for Maine's Future Board."

Shortly thereafter I was called to Augusta for an interview with Department of Conservation Commissioner Pat McGowan, but afterwards I heard no more for over a year. I literally had completely forgotten about the possibility of being appointed when the call came to prepare the paperwork for the hearing on my nomination before the legislature's Joint Standing Committee on Agriculture, Conservation, and Forestry. Also before the committee on the day I stood before it was Leon Gorman, retired head of L.L. Bean and a leader of that iconic Maine family. Leon, completing his first term on the Land for Maine's Future Board, had been nominated for a second term. Before the legislative committee that day too was southern Maine real estate developer Diane Doyle, like me up for a first term on the board.

Little did I realize then that I was destined to serve through the best and the worst of times for the Land for Maine's Future Program and that Leon and Diane would be colleagues whose counsel and example would be among the very best and the most valued by me. I would find Leon a profoundly wise board member, in general quiet but absolutely worth listening to when he spoke. Diane and I would bring our very different experiences with land to bear on Land for Maine's Future Board decisions in ways that I think enhanced for each of us the positions that we took. Developer and conservationist but each an outdoor enthusiast, Diane and I learned from each other and cooperated closely. In our second terms we were to be the only holdovers on the board from the previous administration after Paul LePage became Governor and began showing his hostility to Land for Maine's Future. Through what became the worst of times for the Land for Maine's Future Program despite valiant efforts by newly assigned but demoralized staff, Diane and I tried to support each other through the exasperations. Her final term actually ended ahead of mine, and her last email to me as she left the board concluded, "You're the last of us left."

My time on the Land for Maine's Future Board began on a high note. Executive Director Tim Glidden and Assistant Director Steve Brooke were highly experienced, deeply committed, politically savvy, and not shy about guiding the board when they saw the need. George LaPointe, Commissioner of Marine Resources, served as chairman of the Land for Maine's Future Board. George was knowledgeable and efficient, humorous and personable, and worked wonderfully well in tandem with the talented staff. At the beginning of my tenure George and Tim summoned me to George's office for a very useful orientation and get-to-know-each-other chat, punctuated embarrassingly for me by coughing fits and popping cough drops as I tried to hide an old cold and pretend that I was the picture of good health. I am sure that they thought I was totally toxic and washed their hands vigorously as soon as I departed, but rewarding friendships and effective working relationships began that day.

Staff and board were justly proud of Land for Maine's Future's legacy of accomplishments. Permanent preservation with funding from Land for Maine's Future of properties like Cutler's rugged shorefront, Moosehead Lake's dramatic Mount Kineo, and the Donnell Pond Unit in Hancock County, wherein lies Schoodic Mountain, have made the program consistently popular with Maine voters. Ensuring public access to the Maine outdoors is a matter of much importance to those who value traditional ways of life and to those whose income depends directly or indirectly on attracting visitors to the state. Nothing illustrates the direct tie between conserving wild land and outdoor recreation businesses any better than the hundreds of thousands of acres of forestlands and associated lake and stream frontage preserved in the Downeast Lakes region. The local Grand Lake Stream area businesses that have catered to visiting fishermen for generations have been enthusiastic supporters of this effort, and Land for Maine's Future has been proud to pool its funds with federal and foundation sources and dollars from generous individuals.

Preserving fish habitat is vital for fishermen and preserving terrestrial habitats vital for hunters. Habitat preservation is even more important as an ecological imperative, and the habitat projects brought to the Land for Maine's Future Board for funding assistance by the likes of the Department of Inland Fisheries and Wildlife, The Nature Conservancy, and more localized efforts such as the Pleasant River Wildlife Foundation have been outstanding.

In the working waterfront program the legislature handed the Land for Maine's Future Program responsibility for something so innovative that it has been a first for the nation. This became clear as real estate appraisers struggled with how to appraise permanent use restrictions on fish piers and associated buildings, there being little in the way of precedent or useful model. What started as a pilot effort has proven its worth, and the working waterfront program has secured vital waterfront for commercial fishing purposes in towns the length of the coast and provided fishing families, fish businesses, and fish cooperatives with sometimes critically needed capital that they have been able to plow back into their businesses.

Helping pay for water access sites for the general public, Land for Maine's Future has provided another appreciated service. In a state with so many wonderful bays, rivers, lakes, and ponds, accessing them for purposes of recreation and harvesting aquatic resources is a matter of great import, especially in the face of the heavy private demand for waterfront property, which too often results in closing off places that people have long used to get to the shore.

Why the purchase of conservation easements on Maine farmland is so popular as a Land for Maine's Future endeavor was brought home to me during a July visit by the entire Land for Maine's Future Board to Brunswick's Crystal Spring Farm. Its selling organic produce to the public attracts up to 800 cars on summer Saturday mornings, the owner told us! Maine people increasingly value access to healthy, locally grown foods and, as voters, are eager to approve bonds to preserve farmland and thereby help farms stay in business.

As I joined the Land for Maine's Future Board and began actively participating in its meetings and committees, I realized more than I had before what a justifiably proud tradition I was now part of. The government and people of Maine looked to us to analyze the merits of proposed new projects very carefully and to ensure that public funds entrusted to us were spent as wisely as possible. Certainly, board and staff members going back to inception had done an outstanding job as evidenced by a remarkable and lengthy list of conserved properties. When I listened at meetings to many of the longer-serving board members and to the staff, I was impressed by the depth of their knowledge—of Maine land and people, of prioritizing potential projects, of real estate transaction details and hurdles, of appraising, and of land conservation techniques. I was equally impressed by their dedication to make absolutely the best decisions possible.

I quickly understood that the public trust placed in me required serious dedication to trying to perform my role as a board member as thoughtfully and effectively as I could. In my mind I found that deciding on the expenditure of public funds took my sense of responsibility to a new level, the diligent exercise of which I found I much enjoyed. Certainly, some of my colleagues in the original group with which I served seemed more knowledgeable and dedicated to the program than others, but the overall level of expertise and commitment was high. Meetings were looked forward to, and I often stayed late after adjournment to pursue matters of interest with fellow board members and staff.

Within a few months of my appointment in 2010 to a second term, the best of times rapidly went to the worst of times. The Tea Party era had arrived. Even in a smooth transition from one governor's administration to the next, five of the eleven members of the Land for Maine's Future Board would usually change, for five were heads of state agencies and six were members of the public. That is a large change for any committee to experience all at once. The problem in 2011 was compounded by several of the members from the public reaching the end of their maximum service of two four-year terms. Then all staff except one left too for reasons of attractive job opportunities, retirement, and perhaps distaste at what they foresaw coming.

With so much loss of experience and institutional knowledge all at once, Governor LePage displayed a major management failure in losing one experienced person unnecessarily. Bucky Owen was one of Land for Maine's Future's most experienced, knowledgeable, and wisest board members. Retired from the University of Maine wildlife faculty, a hunter and outdoor enthusiast, a former Commissioner of the Department of Inland Fisheries and Wildlife who as Commissioner had served on the Land for Maine's Future Board at that time too, and an active participant in nonprofit land conservation work, Bucky was concluding only his first term as a member from the public when Governor LePage assumed office. Bucky was willing to be reappointed. The Governor let him go, nonetheless, and Land for Maine's Future suffered even more turnover within a very short period of time than was necessary.

George LaPointe in my view had been an outstanding chairman. With the new administration taking over, he was no longer Commissioner of the Department of Marine Resources and lost his seat on the Land for Maine's Future Board. Although the Land for Maine's Future Program would seem to be bipartisan, the new Governor looked for a Republican, not experience with conservation, in choosing a replacement for George. He turned to Don Marean, who although appointed by Democratic Governor Baldacci, may have been the only Republican on the Land for Maine's Future Board as Baldacci's term came to an end. Don, a former legislator, in his short time on the board to that point had always been quiet and self-effacing in regard to his knowledge about Maine land conservation and Land for Maine's Future processes. He did possess, though, dedication to the mission, political know-how, and a willingness to tackle the host of problems caused by so much turnover. As chairman Don truly earned my respect before he resigned to make a successful run for the legislature. He and I unfortunately found many situations about which to commiserate as Land for Maine's Future struggled to get its feet under itself again.

⁂

With the Governor's blasting state employees in his inaugural address and later publicly calling mid-level state management "corrupt," morale in Augusta plummeted. Bringing Tea Party attitudes about government and spending to the governorship, Paul LePage made no effort to provide funding for a new director of Land for Maine's Future following Tim Glidden's departure for the presidency of Maine Coast Heritage Trust. Jody Harris, reportedly holding down two other what should have been full-time jobs within the State Planning Office, was assigned to oversee the Land for Maine's Future Program. No doubt struggling around the clock to keep up, she held the fort with considerable skill until she not surprisingly exited when she found opportunity in the private sector, adding yet more turnover turmoil.

The staff under Jody's oversight consisted of veteran Collin Therrien and, newly assigned from elsewhere in the State Planning Office, Sam Morris and Tom Miragliuolo, who had to learn as they went. Leaderless after Jody departed, the three did an excellent job of trying to carry out program tasks. I found myself making a real effort to compliment them regularly, but I knew from their demeanors and occasional flashes of emotion that they faced trying circumstances.

Signs of program leadership began to return with the arrival back from a state agency job in Michigan of Ed Meadows, once Maine's Commissioner of Conservation. Back on the Maine state payroll he initially had time for little more than loose oversight of the Land for Maine's Future staff members, telling me that they were going to have to be "self-directed," a concept that I found difficult to accept as an effective way to run a program. We on the board and the staff needed to know who was the boss. The staff leadership finally improved drastically when, following the merger of the Department of Conservation and the Department of Agriculture and the moving of Land for Maine's Future to the merged department from the discontinued State Planning Office, Ed Meadows had time to become acting director. Then, even better, funding for the director position was restored, and Ed became director. Experienced with land matters and politically skilled, he was a worthy successor to Tim Glidden now that he could give the program his full attention.

The inexperienced board faced its own struggles, certainly made worse by the prolonged lack of a full-time program director. Soon after we had so much turnover, we faced a new round of proposals. The board assembled in July 2011 to allocate funds. Although not badly handled, the process of scoring projects, nominating projects for funding, and determining allocations went noticeably less smoothly with more aggravations than three years earlier, but there were few of us left from before to note the difference.

For me, the worst was the executive session of the board that July afternoon to determine just how many dollars to allocate to each project. It was hot in that little upstairs room, and people grew more and more tired as the discussion went on seemingly interminably. My understanding of the process for decision-making led to a sticking point. The scoring committee, which I chaired, provided scores from a complex scoring system to the nominating committee. The scoring process is designed to be as objective and fair as possible, but subjectivity and compromise cannot help but creep in. In the times that I have served on the scoring committee, the credibility of the scores by themselves has been weakened, in my opinion, by the fact that the scoring committee does all the scoring in one day, as a practical matter probably necessary. That makes for a long day. With an increasingly weary committee rushing to conclude as the afternoon progresses, there is the risk of afternoon scoring's being less thoughtful than in the morning. There is one safeguard in that either at the end of the day or subsequently the scoring committee, before considering scores final, makes a comparison of scores to satisfy itself that each project's score relative to other projects' scores seems appropriate. Adjustments are made as seem necessary.

Final scores go to a different committee of the board, the nominating committee. My understanding has always been that although scores may be the most important single factor for the nominating committee to consider, its role is to weigh other factors too. Otherwise, there would be no need for a nominating committee. Some parts of the state may have seen too little funding from Land for Maine's Future. Some projects, although excellent, may not fit the scoring system as well as others. It may be highly desirable to include in the mix of funded projects small projects close to population centers even if they do not score as high as grander projects. The nominating committee can weigh such factors and then recommend to the full board a dollar amount for each project and can recommend projects not to fund at all.

In 2011 the nominating committee came to the full board with recommendations based virtually entirely on scores and with more faith in the quality of the scores than I, even as chair of the scoring committee, thought warranted. Through a long afternoon arguments went back and forth—ironically the nominating committee arguing for the scoring and I, at least, arguing for less reliance on the scores and more on other factors.

That afternoon I came to appreciate my new colleague on the board Chandler Woodcock, Governor LePage's Commissioner of Inland Fisheries and Wildlife. He and I were the principal antagonists in the argument about reliance on scores. Chandler said that he had been a teacher, and for him a D is a D and an A an A. The A's should be funded. I pointed out what I thought were important other factors in regard to certain projects, and I made my case that some of the scores had been developed by a tired committee in a rush to get through the scoring afternoon. In general, I made little headway with my mostly new fellow board members, although I did succeed in getting three projects added to the list to be funded. What really struck me, though, was that as soon as we adjourned and stood up from the table, Chandler came right over to me, shook my hand, and said, "Ben, you did a great job presenting your case!" That is a fine way to treat people and build relationships.

I always enjoyed seeing Chandler. Four years later, as I ended my time on the board during terrible turmoil caused by the Governor's hostility to Land for Maine's Future and the failure, in my opinion, of the commissioners on the board to stand up adequately for the program's integrity, Chandler took me aside after my last meeting and thanked me for having been understanding of the vise in which the commissioners were caught.

꩜

The allocations of funding to specific projects that we made that afternoon in 2011 were not legal commitments to provide the funding within a specific time frame, but they were moral commitments by the Land for Maine's Future Board on behalf of the State of Maine to make the funding available for closing as soon as all the steps of due diligence, including approval of appraisals, was completed. That is the way that the Land for Maine's Future Program had always operated. Funds are allocated after voters have approved the bond issue. Not infrequently, property sellers are people making retirement plans. That has been particularly true of farmers selling conservation easements on working farms. Many sellers have been generous in agreeing to the lengthy time under contract that buyers seeking government funds require. Sellers make plans for their lives based on the allocations, and applicants—government and nonprofit entities—invest great amounts of time and money in pursuing projects. Another aspect of government funding is that frequently applicants for Land for Maine's Future funding also seek funds from federal grant programs. These often have deadlines for closings, and Land for Maine's Future's being prepared to close within the federal deadlines is necessary to prevent possible loss of federal grants. Delays can be hugely costly and, at times, emotionally very challenging.

When we made the 2011 funding allocations, Paul LePage had already been governor for six months, yet his administration gave us no warning that he might indefinitely delay the sale of the bonds necessary to have cash available for closings. We later were to learn that is exactly what he was going to do. He was to refuse to sell bonds, despite such sale being authorized by the voters, with no definite answer about when bond sales would resume. I remember at a board meeting the implications of this sinking in on one of the Governor's own appointees to the Land for Maine's Future Board, new chairman Bill Vail, a man with significant state government experience himself. I admired his publicly voicing dismay at how government's failure to follow through on commitments undercuts public trust in government. The morale of staff and at least some board members plummeted.

We struggled on, burdened by inexperience on both the staff and board and no knowledge of when enough money would again be available to close all approved projects. We also suffered from at least one board member's extremely negative way of participating, perhaps encouraged by the Governor. The board members who were state agency heads continued to be much more hesitant to speak their minds than had been the people in the same roles in the previous governor's administration. This hesitancy was captured at one meeting when a commissioner explained to laughter his silence on an issue under discussion, "I would rather be a commissioner than an ex-commissioner."

How much control was Governor LePage really trying to exert? There were indications that some of the new board members had been given instructions at the times of their nominations. In contrast, no one had ever given me any instructions as to what was expected or what to push. One indication of the desire to control may have been evidenced by the lack of gender and age diversity in the Governor's appointments, dots that I did not connect for a long time. Publicly on several occasions I pointed out that when I had joined the board, there were four women and seven men. Some of that board when I first joined were certainly no older than their forties. All of Governor LePage's appointees were men and mostly in their sixties and even seventies. Whether one of his state agency heads on the board was younger than fifty I am not sure, but certainly no others of his appointees were.

When Diane Doyle's second term ended, there were no women among my colleagues on the board. By then the board had been reduced in size from eleven to nine, and of us nine gray-haired men three had been in the same fraternity at the University of Maine within a year of each other. I was having lunch with a longtime friend one day and commenting on my disbelief that in the twenty-first century the Land for Maine's Future Board had no women and no relatively young members despite its major role in conserving the Maine out-of-doors. Said she, "The Governor does not want diversity." In response to my asking why she replied, "Because then he loses control." What terrible misdirection of a government supposedly of the people, by the people, and for the people.

My frustration at the lack of diversity boiled over at the 2014 meeting at which we allocated the funds for the latest round of projects. I launched into a somewhat emotional tirade on the need for a board more representative of the Maine population and certainly one with women and some younger members. At least three women from state agencies were sitting behind me in the room, and I hoped as I ranted that they were silently cheering me on. The oldest member of the board was sitting right next to me and immediately interjected that he had no use for mere "political correctness." I surprised myself by being able to think fast and answer with the example of my being much influenced on the priority of a project under discussion by comments from one of the staff, who is much younger than I am. The particular project included one of Maine's best rock-climbing cliffs, and this staff member was better able than I, perhaps because of his being from a younger generation, to spot the importance of the project. The lack of diversity on the Land for Maine's Future Board appalled me.

Others too thought that Maine was living through the worst of times for the Land for Maine's Future Program. At one point the press began to publicize the situation, and I received some calls. At the low point of my discouragement I was sitting in the cockpit of our boat in St. John, Virgin Islands, waiting to cast off the mooring when my cell phone rang. It was a reporter from the Maine media. For forty-five minutes I poured out my frustrations, words which I was to see in print when I returned home. I have never liked being in the role of a complainer, but I had come to feel like "Complainer in Chief" for Land for Maine's Future. I said that to some of my conservation colleagues around the state and received universal encouragement to keep it up.

I erroneously thought that light was finally beginning to show at the end of the tunnel as Ed Meadows took hold as acting director and then director; the Governor agreed that bonds could be sold; authorization was had to request a new round of proposals; and, importantly, staff and board had had time to learn on the job. Certainly, some of the serious problems remained, but the prospect of Land for Maine's Future regaining its proud place in Maine's conservation world seemed likely. Unfortunately, Ed, for family reasons, decided he must retire as director of Land for Maine's Future. I was sympathetic with Ed's reasons for leaving, but I hated to see the loss of an experienced, skilled hand at the helm just as the program seemed to be finally on the upswing.

The able, well-liked Sarah Demers left the Department of Inland Fisheries and Wildlife to replace Ed, but she arrived to ever more dysfunction. The Governor escalated his efforts to obstruct for his own reasons a program for which the voting public consistently demonstrated strong support. By this time all board members except me had been appointed by Governor LePage, not Baldacci. LePage's appointees Chairman Bill Vail, Jim Gorman, Jim Norris, and Neil Piper strove as hard as I did to keep the program on track with little support from the commissioners on the board. The commissioners seemed saddled with insoluble conflicts of interest—duty to their boss, the Governor; duty to keep their departments functioning as smoothly as possible; duty to themselves and their families to retain their salaries and pensions; and duty to the Land for Maine's Future Board, on which they served. To oppose the Governor's wishes might cause immediate firing. In the original structuring of the board by statute, the legislature probably never anticipated a governor so hostile to the Land for Maine's Future Program and the conflicts of interest that would trigger for commissioners serving on the board.

Serving until replaced, I believe that I probably served longer past the end of my two-term limit than any member of the Land for Maine's Future Board in history, for the Governor went through a period of refusing to appoint anyone to any state board, arguably a dereliction of duty in the job he was being paid to do. Eventually he did replace me, and his appointees except the commissioners also came to the end of their terms and were replaced by others. In the case of the highly experienced Jim Norris, Jim was eager to serve a second term, yet as the Governor had done in letting valuable Bucky Owen go out to pasture, LePage let Jim's experience and wisdom vanish from the Land for Maine's Future Board too. Just as I had been the last one standing of the original group with which I served, Neil Piper was the last one standing of the public members with whom I served. When the Governor's new appointees and the commissioners in 2016 unprecedentedly refused to honor decisions already made by the board and up until then considered to be final, Neil, a man of rectitude and backbone, resigned to protest the political hijacking of this once proud program.

Serving on the Land for Maine's Future Board I truly found a privilege—and in making decisions about taxpayer dollars a serious responsibility. In my early years on the board I was part of an able, experienced, and efficient team. In my latter years the exasperations were substantial, but individually I liked and enjoyed the new people and respected the dedication of almost all to learning as they went and to trying to carry out their duties properly. About the commissioners and what I considered their conflicts of interest, I never could come to a conclusion in my own mind as to how I thought that they should have dealt with the conflicts. The staff worked diligently and well under increasingly difficult circumstances.

What always excites everyone involved with the program are new rounds of projects. When the legislature and voters resume approving bond issues, probably not until there is a different Governor, new rounds can continue and more Maine land can be conserved. Over time more than one staff member has articulated to me the excitement of new rounds by comparing the receipt of proposals for new projects to opening Christmas presents. What has particularly struck me in reading proposals is the sheer number of dedicated people associated with a wide variety of organizations in diverse parts of the state who are working extremely hard at trying to preserve the best of Maine's extraordinary lands.

In 2017 Maine Audubon's newsletter published an excellent piece on Land for Maine's Future by Maine Coast Heritage Trust's outstanding Senior Public Policy Manager, Jeff Romano. The larger land conservation organizations such as Maine Coast Heritage Trust, The Nature Conservancy, and the Trust for Public Land have followed the program very closely, assisted program staff where possible, and worked tirelessly to maintain the support of legislators and the voting public. Jeff Romano has led the charge for Maine Coast Heritage Trust and is an expert on the program, keeping track of statistics and details far better than I have.

In his article for Audubon several of his points especially deserve emphasis. One is that this program, which was established originally under a Republican administration, has continued to receive funding in years when Democratic and Independent governors were in office. A

2015 statewide public opinion survey, according to Jeff, found that 84 percent of Maine registered voters supported continued funding for the program. Especially interesting to me is his reported statistic that Land for Maine's Future Program's ground-breaking working waterfront program to protect commercial fishing access to the ocean has benefited 1,280 fishing families and more than 630 fishing vessels—this benefit to commercial fishing interests on top of all the land conservation achievements.

There is no doubt in my mind that the Land for Maine's Future Program is one of the best ways for Maine people to continue to invest in protecting the state's quality of place, so important for so many reasons. The voters have a record of being enthusiastic. I only hope that politicians eventually will again provide the necessary support to revitalize and improve the program.

18

SCHOODIC TO SCHOODIC

"Schoodic," a wonderful-sounding word, has come into both my sailing and conservation activities in numerous ways. I have described the annual excitement at heading east around Schoodic Point when starting a sailing cruise to the exceptional cruising grounds of eastern Maine. The word has also been a near constant over many years of my conservation life—Schoodic Point, Schoodic Island, Schoodic District of Acadia National Park, Schoodic Head, Schoodic Peninsula, Schoodic Mountain, Schoodic Bog, Schoodic Institute, even Schoodic to Schoodic. What does this intriguing word mean?

It certainly has a Native American derivation. I have seen varying definitions from multiple sources. *Auke* reportedly means "place." The Daughters of Liberty in their 1904 *Historical Researches of Gouldsboro, Maine* stated that for the Passamaquoddies *Skut-Auke*, from which "Schoodic" may derive, means fire place or land that has burned. Local historian Allen Workman in his fine history *Schoodic Point* suggests that the word may come from the Native American *esquodek*, meaning "'the end' of land to be navigated." David Cook in his *Above the Gravel Bar: The Native Canoe Routes of Maine* has stated, referring to a stream elsewhere in Maine, that *schoodic* there means "trout place." That has consistency to what is stated in an appendix to Thoreau's *The Maine Woods*—that *schoot* means "rush," and with *auke* meaning place, *schoot-auke* or "schoodic" means "place where water rushes." That could indeed be a trout stream.

There is even a nautical connection made in the same appendix to Thoreau—that "schooner" may derive from Native American words *scoot* and *scoon*. Perhaps a schooner is a boat that scoots or rushes—goes fast. Some schooners indeed do go fast under the right conditions. Did I ever sail on a schooner to Schoodic? Yes. On one day of the New York Yacht Club Cruise in 1963 when I was crewing on that great racing schooner *Nina*, the Schoodic bell buoy was a turning mark of the race course.

I credit Acadia National Park planner John Kelly with galvanizing my recognition of the conservation significance of the mainland of the Schoodic area. He also educated me to the importance of "corridors" in habitat preservation. We were in a meeting in a small room sided in dark, old varnished boards in downtown Winter Harbor's landmark Hammond Hall, now a center for arts and performances. As we looked at a map, John pointed out the large areas of undeveloped and lightly developed forests, wetlands, lakes, ponds, and bogs stretching away to the north from the Schoodic District of Acadia National Park. The Park land forms the end of the massive peninsula south of U.S. Route 1, about which Louise Dickinson Rich so charmingly wrote in her book *The Peninsula*. She called this extensive peninsula "the Gouldsboro Peninsula," and indeed the geographically large town of Gouldsboro comprises much of it. On the west is the drama of Frenchman Bay. On the south and southeast is the sometimes brutal Atlantic Ocean, and on the eastern side of the upper portion of this land mass is the much gentler Gouldsboro Bay. The southern part of the peninsula lies in the geographically smaller town of Winter Harbor, and it is this final, rugged protrusion into the Gulf of Maine that is commonly referred to as the Schoodic Peninsula.

What John underscored that day in Hammond Hall was that all the undeveloped land provides a connection for animal and plant species between the ocean at Acadia National Park and the Maine North Woods. Sixteen miles north of Acadia's Schoodic Point and north of Route 1 is Schoodic Mountain within the Donnell Pond Unit of the State's Public Reserved Lands. The more than 14,000-acre Donnell Pond Unit, consisting of hills and ponds very similar in landform to Mount Desert Island, can reasonably be considered the beginning of the North Woods. Nowhere on the East Coast except eastern Maine does forest still meet the sea with just minimal disruptions from roads and development—"truly unique" in the words of longtime Forest Society of Maine president Alan Hutchinson.

Within the Schoodic District of Acadia is the high ground of

Schoodic Head. From its summit facing north one can enjoy the long sweep of forested landscape toward Schoodic Mountain and the others of the Black Hills in the distance. One day Acadia's Superintendent Sheridan Steele stood there with Pat McGowan, Commissioner of Conservation in the days before the Maine Department of Conservation was combined with the Department of Agriculture. They admired below them the long expanse of woods to the north with shimmering bays and islands on each side. As they stood there with their backs to Schoodic Point and their eyes on Schoodic Mountain, Pat exclaimed, "Schoodic to Schoodic!"

In that three-word, catchy phrase Pat caught the essence of the ecological corridor that John Kelly had described. The phrase remains a useful term to refer to the landscape-scale conservation vision that now continues northward eight miles beyond Schoodic Mountain to include The Nature Conservancy's 11,600-acre Spring River Lake Preserve abutting the Donnell Pond Unit. Schoodic to Schoodic was to take much of my time for several years, and it continues to provide a framework for some of my own conservation interests and pursuits.

I made it my business to learn more about ecological corridors and why they are important. In previous land conservation work I had not been guided by the concept of connectivity within the landscape; in fact, I was largely ignorant of the importance of connecting habitat blocks in order to preserve biodiversity. I began reading what I could find. The title of one particularly helpful book illustrates the focus of that quest for knowledge: *Corridor Ecology, the Science and Practice of Linking Landscapes for Biodiversity Conservation.*

Why are corridors important? Large blocks of undeveloped land are increasingly being fragmented in coastal Maine and everywhere else. Houses, roads, shopping centers, industrial facilities, schools, all these needs of mankind require land. These requirements are often met by developing what previously had been part of a large block of intact habitat for wildlife and plants. As I earlier recounted in mention of the effort to help Frenchman Bay Conservancy secure the 400 acres abutting the Gouldsboro Unit of Coastal Islands National Wildlife Refuge, then refuge manager Charlie Blair had strongly encouraged me because with so much habitat fragmentation along the Maine coast, the remaining blocks of forest habitat are ever more vital.

Corridors connecting blocks of habitat play an important role by providing routes for species that can use them to move between blocks. Such species may thus avoid debilitating effects of genetic isolation and, hopefully, survive in the face of environmental changes and natural disasters that may have damaged one block but not others to which there are migratory connections. Corridors with a north–south axis and, in the Northern Hemisphere, a rising elevation as they trend to the north—like Schoodic to Schoodic—seem especially significant in this time of trying to increase species resilience in the face of a warming climate. The Schoodic to Schoodic corridor is doubly important, for it not only leads north toward higher latitude but also provides a path southward toward the coast, which the ocean keeps cooler than the interior in summer.

John Kelly had pointed out the significance of an ecological connection between the ocean at Schoodic Point and the North Woods. Pat McGowan came up with the inspired name for that corridor of "Schoodic to Schoodic." Frenchman Bay Conservancy, the local land trust for eastern Hancock County, latched on to the concept and under the leadership of then executive director Barb Welch made conservation of critical natural lands in the Schoodic to Schoodic area a major component of the organization's strategic plan. The vision includes maximizing contiguity but also conserving "stepping stones," non-contiguous habitat parcels that may be expandable and connectable as future opportunities arise. Certainly, birds, insects, and many plant seeds can migrate between stepping stones.

❧

About the time that Frenchman Bay Conservancy had made Schoodic to Schoodic a strategic plan priority, various issues and opportunities in the corridor area were arising, and representatives of interested organizations and government agencies began meeting to discuss these. Somehow I was included even though at the time I was not representing any of the entities. We all looked to Frenchman Bay Conservancy for leadership, for it was the only one at the time whose interests clearly spanned the entire geographic extent of the corridor. Later Maine Coast Heritage Trust would focus on the entire geography too.

The Conservancy conceived of a Schoodic to Schoodic coordinating committee and asked me to chair it. So began a process of planning, identification of opportunities and threats, pursuit of some land purchases, and analysis of how to respond to perceived threats. Entities participating in the coordinating committee in addition to Frenchman Bay Conservancy were Maine Coast Heritage Trust, Friends of Acadia, the Forest Society of Maine, Acadia National Park, the U.S. Fish and Wildlife Service, the Maine Bureau of Parks and Lands, and the Maine Department of Inland Fisheries and Wildlife. Frenchman Bay Conservancy retained Muskie School graduate student Misha Mytar, formerly with Blue Hill Heritage Trust and subsequently with Maine Coast Heritage Trust, to prepare a preliminary report in 2007 on the validity of the corridor concept, lands within the corridor of particular importance, and the results of her interviews with conservation professionals, landowners, and other community members. Misha's report remains a useful and thought-provoking reference document.

As often the case, there was an elephant in the living room—or, rather, in the Schoodic to Schoodic corridor—and it was a very large elephant indeed. Its story deserves a book, but here I will summarize the long tale only briefly. The elephant was the 3,200 acres, mostly in Winter Harbor but some in Gouldsboro, which belonged to the Modena family of Milan, Italy, and abutted Acadia National Park. The property spans almost the entire width of the Schoodic Peninsula, and too much and poorly sited development would destroy the ecological integrity of the Schoodic to Schoodic corridor and its utility for fauna and flora movement.

In the first decade of Maine Coast Heritage Trust existence we were aware that much of what later came to be owned by the Modenas belonged to the Chafee family of Rhode Island political fame and with a strong summer presence in Sorrento. We at Maine Coast Heritage Trust had much contact with various members of the Chafee clan and

certainly floated the idea of a conservation easement. What later came
to seem absolute blindness on our part, though, is that in the 1970s we
failed to see the conservation priority of this large forested parcel. We
were then focused on islands, headlands, and similar prominent shoreline features. The property's mainland shorefront forms the eastern
side of the outlet of Mill Stream but is largely hidden from view from
the harbor at Winter Harbor by off-lying Sargent and Norris Islands
and a small peninsula to the north of them unless one ventures into
the delightful narrow waterway north of Acadia National Park's Frazer
Point, where Dianna and I often row and paddleboard. The conservation importance that we had failed to see in the 1970s during Chafee
ownership was underscored by fifteen years beginning about 1995 of
considering the unprotected Modena lands the single greatest threat to
Acadia National Park.

After extensive debate within the Chafee family the property had
been put up for sale about 1980. The Chafees wanted to be careful to
whom they sold, but title to the land vanished into an obscure holding
company with a New York address. Years later local realtor Vance Gray
told me that he had met the buyers at the time of the sale but that they
were adamant that they remain anonymous.

The next nearly fifteen years passed quietly. Then it became urgent
to find out who the owners were. A forester had been hired to arrange
a major timber harvest on the land. The Park entrance road passes
through the property, and the southern property line is very close to the
Schoodic Head overlook in Acadia, from which much of the extraordinary view to the north is of these then-Modena-owned forests stretching away toward Schoodic Mountain in the distance. Also, the property
comes to about 120 feet of the Park exit road. Park Superintendent Paul
Haertel very much wanted to encourage the owners to consider the
Park viewshed in making harvesting plans.

I called one of the Chafee family only to learn that they never had
been able to determine who had bought their property. In fact, I learned
that the sellers had provided financing and that at one point payments
were late. Two of the Chafee clan decided to visit the New York City
address of the holding company to which the town sent tax bills. What

did they report finding? A blank door with nothing behind it.

After word of the planned timber harvest leaked out, Ken Olson, president of Friends of Acadia, finally ferreted out the identity of the actual owners—Bruno and Vittorio Modena, a father and son from Milan. Discussions about the harvest did take place between the Park and representatives of the owners. Also, I am told that major Maine timberland owners pressured the forester to be careful next to a national park, fearing that public outcry could lead to the legislature's enacting more stringent harvest regulations for the entire state. The land was cut and cut hard, but a forester friend subsequently commented to me that he thought a decent job had been done of protecting aesthetics.

Following Paul Haertel's retirement, Sheridan Steele arrived as the new Superintendent of Acadia National Park. Mike Blaney, Acadia's hugely knowledgeable lands manager, lost no time in convincing Sheridan that the uncertain future of the Modena lands posed a very serious threat to the national park. I was on the Acadia National Park Advisory Commission at the time, and Mike indeed did well at keeping people's attention focused on this threat at Schoodic.

The Modenas proved very hard people with whom to communicate. At one point they commented about plans for 2,000 homes. Later came word that planning consultants were being hired to begin preparing development plans for villas, two hotels, a golf course, even an airstrip. Maps and proposals began appearing for what they ludicrously referred to as an "eco-resort," which included such environmentally disastrous amenities as a golf course in the wetlands, an airstrip in the forest of the Schoodic to Schoodic ecological corridor, and an "aquacenter" on the unspoiled, wild Sargent Island.

Years of energetic effort by the conservation community ensued in a concerted effort to persuade the Modenas to sell. Strong leadership for this effort engaging many of the organizations participating in the Schoodic to Schoodic coordinating committee came from Sheridan as Park superintendent, from Friends of Acadia's Ken Olson, and from

Dianna, who then chaired Ken's board. Maine Coast Heritage Trust participated in discussions and provided information but chose not to jump into a leadership role until the saga's later years. At times Governor Baldacci's office was involved too, as was Commissioner of Conservation Pat McGowan.

Sheridan had worked with The Conservation Fund in Colorado and had high regard for its capabilities. I was no longer representing The Conservation Fund in Maine, but Sheridan asked me to reestablish my relationship with the Fund specifically to try to arrange a purchase by it.

The cast of characters in this drama was extraordinary—prominent philanthropists, National Park Service personnel, state officials, many conservation leaders from the nonprofits, a revolving door of consultants to the owners, and, finally, the elusive owners in Milan. Despite many meetings with various representatives of the owners and even two or three times when people working on this did succeed in getting hold of one of the Modenas on the telephone, we got nowhere. In 2005 I made an offer on behalf of The Conservation Fund to the American consultant who was the senior representative of the owners and, that going nowhere, then arranged for him to receive an offer from another philanthropic source. These were generous offers. Clearly, the owners had no interest in selling, seeing more long-run profit from executing the crystallizing plans for a so-called "eco-resort." I often said to Sheridan that the two of us would be dead before the Modena situation was resolved.

To my astonishment and the surprise of all involved, the solution fell out of the sky. Sheridan finally had succeeded in having a face-to-face meeting with Vittorio Modena, and it did seem that at last he and his father might consider selling—perhaps spurred by the Great Recession, which changed the plans of so many. An anonymous and extraordinarily generous conservation buyer materialized in a conversation with Sheridan. Lyme Timber, a New Hampshire–based conservation-oriented timber management and investing company, and Maine Coast Heritage Trust with help from Friends of Acadia then swung into action to help the buyer under the name Schoodic Woods LLC complete the purchase in December 2011 and work toward its public-spirited goals.

The southern half of the land, which lies south of the east–west Route 186 across the peninsula, is rough, hilly land dominated by red spruce, white cedar, and jack pine that is still recovering from the hard cutting in the mid-1990s. There the buyer constructed bicycle trails and a campground for visitors to Schoodic before passing ownership through the National Park Foundation to Acadia. The buyer is working with conservation interests on a plan for the northern half, ecologically perhaps the most important part because of extensive wetlands. Efforts to protect other lands in the corridor continue, all this work critical to the integrity of the Schoodic District of Acadia, the welfare of the local communities, and realizing the dream of the Schoodic to Schoodic corridor of protected natural lands.

19

PESSIMISM AND HOPE
IN A FAST-CHANGING WORLD

A s the little Cape Air plane lifted off the runway in Boston, I was excited as I always am when returning home. The pilot banked to the right and steadied on course for the Bar Harbor Airport in Trenton. It was a spectacularly beautiful clear morning in mid-March 2015. Dianna and I had been sailing for six weeks in the Virgin Islands. Because of a Land for Maine's Future Board meeting the following week we were on our way back to Maine during one of the coldest winters in many years. Dianna joked that she deserved an award for leaving the warmth and outdoor life of the tropics for my conservation obligations.

I had a book to read during the flight, but the view to the left of the aircraft was too good. We passed over the extensive salt marshes of the northern Massachusetts coast. I could see where the Merrimack River flows into the ocean, followed soon by the Piscataqua separating New Hampshire from Maine and, closer to our course, the off-lying small archipelago of the Isles of Shoals. Off to the west the southern Maine beaches passed and Biddeford Pool, Prouts Neck, and Cape Elizabeth at the entrance to Casco Bay. There Maine's island-studded coast commences, and I began to test my memory of island names gained from years of cruising among the islands and my endlessly studying the chart-covered wall in the original Maine Coast Heritage Trust office overlooking Frenchman Bay.

Dianna was seated in the vacant co-pilot seat. Over her shoulder rugged Monhegan Island appeared ahead, one place that I have never landed but have sailed past often. Muscongus Bay passed by inshore, and we were quickly at the entrance to vast Penobscot Bay. Over Vinalhaven, white from a light snow the previous day, I peered down into Perry Creek, so often a favorite anchorage for us and a place of memorable hikes on the lands surrounding the creek, which have been preserved thanks to effective work by both the Vinalhaven Land Trust and Maine Coast Heritage Trust. Seal Bay on Vinalhaven's southeast shore, a wonderful place to explore in a rowboat or on a paddleboard, slid under our right wing. Isle au Haut lay just beyond across East Penobscot Bay. There was Duck Harbor Mountain, a fancy name for a modest hill which we have climbed many times, in the Isle au Haut District of Acadia National Park.

The plane bored on through the sky over Deer Isle and straight for Brooklin. Below spread all those treasured islands at the eastern end of Eggemoggin Reach and beloved Center Harbor, empty of boats at this time of year. To the left clearly showed the great hayfields of our Meadow Brook Farm with a light covering of snow. The hills of Mount Desert Island rose very prominently ahead now, just to the right of our course as we crossed Blue Hill Bay and zeroed in on the runway. As we descended, Eastern Bay at the head of Frenchman Bay stretched off to the right, and around the farthest point of land visible on Mount Desert we knew was our house and waiting cat. The wheels touched down. What a spectacular and invigorating way to come home!

A prime advantage of leaving Maine is one's enhanced appreciation of it upon return. On this trip we had again viewed the sad and rapid deterioration of the appeal of the British Virgin Islands. Enormous amounts of money have poured in to those once magnificent islands to build over-the-top resorts, super-luxurious private villas on more and more cliffs, facilities for huge cruise ships, and marinas to attract even the largest yachts of international oligarchs. At one time it seemed the British Virgin Islands government was conscious that heedless, uncontrolled development would destroy the goose that laid its golden egg—spectacular scenery, charming quiet, crystal-clear waters, and pristine coral reefs. Tourist development was needed, but only to be undertaken slowly and with great care. Instead, the gold is there but in the form of enormously deleterious impact on those very qualities that made the islands special. (Above written prior to September 2017 Hurricane Irma devastation in Virgin Islands.)

Change in Maine fortunately has come much more slowly so far and under tighter controls. Thank goodness we have the highly effective conservation programs of so many government and nonprofit entities and, in general, a citizenry long supportive of environmental protection despite appalling lack of commitment of some recent elected officials and political appointees.

In this era when so many people have bucket lists of places they wish to visit and trips they want to take, I find air travel sufficiently unpleasant as to discourage trips. With the attitude that Maine has what I need, I immediately wrote down a comment that I heard on Maine Public Radio. I was listening to a talk show with panelists who had done major long-distance hiking, such as Georgia to Maine on the Appalachian Trail. A panelist commented that he probably would not do more of those trips, saying, "We have more than enough majesty here in Maine to keep me happy." A kindred soul, for sure.

⁓⁂

When I first became engaged in Maine conservation, I certainly did not realize how drastically different the world and all our lives would be forty-plus years later. For me, though, my worries about the state of the world late in the second decade of the twenty-first century eerily mirror earlier thinking. While I was studying for my Masters of Business Administration degree at Dartmouth's Tuck School, *The Limits to Growth* was published in 1972. The last three words of the subtitle, *A Report for The Club of Rome's Project on the Predicament of Mankind*, say it all—"Predicament of Mankind."

This book garnered enormous world-wide attention when it came out, especially so at Dartmouth, where lead authors Drs. Donnella and Dennis Meadows taught. They presented to one of my classes the report's thesis that population and development trends, if unchecked, would cause the planet to run out of the resources on which mankind depends. At the time, newly married and with an infant daughter, I worried that by the end of the 1970s the world would be a far less desirable place to be than it was in the early years of the decade.

Life on Earth was not upended that rapidly, as it turned out, and for a time the vociferous critics of *The Limits to Growth* claimed vindication. New oil reserves were discovered; pollution-control tech-nologies and regulations improved; agricultural productivity increased; and family size in the developed world decreased. Optimists put huge faith in technology to get past seeming limits. I have always thought, however, that even if the ultimate limits of the planet would not be reached as fast as the Club of Rome projected, the concept of planetary limits to endless growth is absolutely on target. In the 1970s I did not anticipate the explosive economic growth of China, in particular, nor the massive expansion of the middle classes around the world with their understandable desires to consume as greedily as we Americans do. I did expect, though, continued rapid population growth in many parts of the world, and that, of course, has happened and will continue to happen at least for many decades longer.

Now we seemingly have limits to growth squarely in our faces again and this time even more menacingly. In 1972 I never heard, for exam-ple, that the ongoing increases in greenhouse gas generation in grow-ing economies might push the world past an irreversible tipping point causing global warming beyond human ability to adapt. Global warm-ing with its interrelationships with overpopulation, poverty, unchecked economic greed, human migration, radicalism, civil conflict, terrorism, and species extinctions now hangs over us. We have learned that at best it will be many years before mankind can stop the rise of average temperatures. Adaptation and resilience, the latter a word that I never used to hear, are now essential. So too are rapid advances in a host of critical technologies.

Much influenced by *The Limits to Growth*, I was pessimistic as I left business school and began my conservation career. Now I try to hold at bay a return of that old pessimism about the future, not so much the future during my lifetime but certainly during the expected lifespans of children and grandchildren. I keep much in mind a phrase of the University of Maine's marine researcher Dr. Robert Steneck—that it is important not to "get caught in the cul-de-sac of despair."

I have always thought of myself as a centrist, generally not in favor of extremes and rapid changes. I am concluding, though, that policies based on a middle-of-the-road philosophy to solve interrelated environmental and societal problems are unlikely to bring solutions quickly enough. This is more than a sobering realization; it is, admittedly, frightening. To minimize the ravages on human societies and on nature of pollution, overtaxed ecosystem services, and a warming planet and to reverse the world's growing social inequities require all of us—everywhere including here in Maine—to make major lifestyle adjustments, including drastically reduced use of carbon-based energy.

That here in Maine change has come more slowly than to so many other parts of the world has been an enormous benefit of the decision to make my adult life in this state. The natural world and stunning scenery are still close at hand. Crowds and traffic are still minimal by standards of large urban areas except at peak tourist times. As elsewhere, sprawl has overtaken too much of the land, but in the face of land development pressures Maine's system of federal, state, municipal, and nonprofit land conservation programs has achieved a record of accomplishments that would make any state proud.

Development pressures may accelerate sooner than we have thought, though. In the spring of 2016 I was privileged to meet and chat with climate scientist Dr. Paul Mayewski of the University of Maine's Climate Change Institute. He strongly made the case that within ten years Maine is going to experience significant in-migration of climate refugees from parts of the country even more impacted than here by changes in climate such as increasing periods of heat and drought, stronger storms, and rising sea levels. In Paul's words, Maine is viewed by climate scientists as a "sweet spot." What will that mean regarding greater land development pressures?

Maine's air and freshwater resources seem relatively healthy compared to many other places, although air quality is degraded by industrial emissions from the Midwest, and lakes suffer from pollution and invasive species. Rivers are actually less polluted than when I was young, and removing dams is proving hugely beneficial to fish.

Salt water has its own issues. The decline of salt water fisheries except lobsters has been massively documented and publicized. It began when Europeans first appeared off New England and has continued dramatically during my lifetime. I remember as a young child a relatively productive day handlining for finfish off ledges in Jericho Bay with a local fisherman on his ancient boat, which he was willing to use for day charters. Most people would not bother today. The late Richard Rockefeller, son of Maine Coast Heritage Trust founder Peggy Rockefeller and himself a major figure in the organization's history, once commented to me that his joy in sailing Maine waters had been greatly diminished by knowing how barren was the water under his keel. To me who so much revels in being afloat under sail, that was a troubling new way to think about sailing.

Changes in the Gulf of Maine are now front-page news on a regular basis. Ocean acidification, water warming faster than almost all other water bodies on the planet, declining eelgrass beds, lobsters molting earlier and facing diseases creeping northwards, southern species coming to northern waters—these ocean problems and more spell great uncertainty for the future.

Human values of commitment to community, neighbors, and family for the most part seem to remain relatively strong, but the aging population, limited economic opportunities, and drug use and other social problems, especially in some rural areas, signal ongoing troubles ahead. If the ecological changes in the Gulf of Maine cause the lobster fishery to collapse, seemingly very possible, social and economic changes in many coastal communities could be drastic and, for many people, devastating.

An ever more worrisome environmental change and public health menace in Maine is the arrival and spread of deer ticks. They now carry multiple bacterial diseases, Lyme's being best known, and a scary, only recently publicized virus with no known treatment. Dianna and I have both been treated with antibiotics for Lyme disease, fortunately caught before becoming the long-term type with serious medical repercussions. Time spent in fields and woods now is very different than years ago, given the desirability of wearing long pants tucked into socks, wearing long sleeves, and spraying oneself with insecticide containing DEET. Showering upon coming indoors, checking one's body carefully in the mirror for ticks, and lengthy washing machine and dryer runs on hot settings are all part of everyday life. We have no way of knowing how much more the deer ticks will change life in Maine. I hope for an effective vaccine.

When I joined the original Maine Coast Heritage Trust staff in 1971, we at that organization were focused on the need to counter the diminishing wildness of privately owned coastal islands. Scenery and the psychological rewards of wild places seemed at risk. We thought that we could protect the scenic and natural qualities of Maine islands by encouraging island owners to donate conservation easements, often then called scenic easements, to government agencies, the only entities at that time authorized to hold conservation easements under Maine statutory law.

Many board members thought the need for Maine Coast Heritage Trust would be temporary—accomplish as much as could be achieved with island protection in a few years, then close the doors. We did not foresee that Maine Coast Heritage Trust would in time expand drastically and local land trusts proliferate, acquiring not only easements but ownership of mainland and island properties along with the permanent stewardship burden of those acquisitions. Large amounts of money would have to be raised on an ongoing basis to buy land and easements and to support all the staff and infrastructure essential to holding real estate interests on a large scale. In the 1970s and 1980s we worried about Maine coast lands being loved to death by ever-growing legions of outdoor enthusiasts—more and more pleasure boaters, kayakers, campers, hikers, and cross-country skiers. We did not foresee the days of children's becoming so focused on their digital devices indoors that they might fail to learn to appreciate the natural world outside.

We early recognized the need to try to build broad public support and particularly the support of municipal officials for land conservation, but we did not foresee how land conservation organizations would find that promoting recreation on conservation lands was a critical component of building broad public support and that in making the case for economic benefits of land conservation it would be necessary to go beyond our early efforts at showing possible beneficial fiscal impacts on town budgets. "Economic benefit," drawing dollars into a community and its businesses, would become almost a buzzword phrase among land conservationists, followed even more recently by another such phrase, "community engagement"—involving local people in the management decisions about land's being conserved in their communities. Maine Coast Heritage Trust's 2013 strategic plan made attention-grabbing statements in regard to the need for community support. Said the plan, "Land conservation that is perceived as irrelevant to community needs may become a target of wrath." Alarming to someone like myself who first engaged in land conservation efforts decades ago, the strategic plan also warns, "Indeed the threat is not simply to our future work but also to the integrity of our past successes."

If communities are to continue to be supportive of land conservation efforts, other community needs must be taken into account, requirements such as property tax revenues and land for housing, schools, businesses, landfills, and the other myriad needs of towns and cities. I never used to hear conservationists ask in regard to conserved land, "When is enough enough?" The question was shocking to me when I first heard it from one of my most respected colleagues on the Land for Maine's Future Board, but I clearly understand it now.

Today's land conservation work in government agencies and non-profit organizations is much more based on planning and the analysis of ecosystems, scientific data, economic considerations, and competing community needs for land. Most recently, climate change considerations have become important in conservation planning. Land conservation is much less just seizing available opportunities than when I began. In the nonprofit sector, vastly more people work in land conservation at many more organizations. The field has become a true profession with training available in degree programs at colleges and universities and at courses and conferences organized by conservation organizations themselves. Today's staff members of nonprofit land conservation organizations no longer "wing it" and learn as they go in the way many of us did who began around the time of the original Earth Day.

Far, far more money has been made available in Maine over the decades. More and wealthier philanthropists, foundations, and federal and state funding programs have all made a huge difference, providing dollars on a scale unimaginable in 1970. The Great Recession and unfortunate political developments may have reduced available funds in recent years, but there remain many, many more sources of funds for land conservation than I ever would have anticipated.

In Maine, and I have no doubt in many other states too, the mission of land conservation programs has broadened dramatically. Originally, for example, Maine Coast Heritage Trust just promoted and negotiated conservation easements to be held by other entities. Today it owns and manages a whole system of preserves that function like government parks, offers trips to its preserves, operates a farm where it raises cattle and educates young people about agriculture, and runs a service bureau for all of Maine's land trusts.

The Nature Conservancy has similarly expanded its mission. With a one-man Maine Chapter staff in the early 1970s it opportunistically acquired parcels of open-space value including a number of islands. Later, science would drive its acquisition decisions and lead to large North Woods landholdings with as much acreage as possible. Today a major part of its Maine effort is out in the ocean waters of the Gulf of Maine cooperating with commercial fishing interests in efforts to restore sustainable biological productivity.

Even Acadia National Park has expanded its mission, using its Schoodic Institute–managed Schoodic Education and Research Center to try to make the Park a center for ecological research, nature-based STEM education, citizen science, and training for Americans and foreigners in conservation techniques. What were once relatively simple and highly focused efforts have had to become complex and much more sophisticated in order to try to meet today's enormous challenges.

My own participation in Maine conservation efforts evolved from professional work to a mix of professional and volunteer effort and then to an all-volunteer focus. In my volunteer phase I have recently begun to go beyond the land to seek ways to increase my participation in efforts aimed at protecting the marine environment from the high-tide line to the depths of the Gulf of Maine. Certainly, the sea needs as much protection as the land. Said world-renowned conservationist and oceanographer Dr. Sylvia Earle in a 2015 interview with the Conservation Law Foundation, "Life itself depends on the ocean—and most of life on Earth is under the ocean's surface."

Now I engage in conservation to the extent that I wish, when I wish. Doing so remains hugely satisfying, keeps me in touch with outstanding people, and, hopefully, does some good for Maine. I rarely let it interfere with sailing, though. When friends ask what I have been up to, I often admit that I am almost embarrassed by how much time I spend on the water.

✤

My sailing has evolved too, although the world in which I sail has evolved more. Fortunately, despite Maine's shores having become more built-up with summer homes and harbors more crowded with resident pleasure boats, the scenic character and rejuvenating sense of wildness remain intact in many places. Many favorite cruising anchorages surprisingly have not grown significantly more crowded. On *West Wind* Dianna and I still often find ourselves joyfully alone at night, no doubt partly reflecting what friends in the boat industry have told me for a number of years, that younger people are not buying cruising sailboats any more.

Busy lives, briefer vacations, stagnant middle-class incomes, children committed to organized summer programs, and shifting interest patterns all have taken a toll on desire for sailboats, especially sailboats for overnight cruising. Daysailers sell better than cruising sailboats, and powerboats sell far better than sailboats. Socially prominent yachting centers like Camden and Northeast Harbor now see many more truly huge yachts than when I was young, conspicuous evidence of enormous fortunes made in recent decades, but fortunately these mega yachts rarely are neighbors in harbors where we anchor when cruising.

Outside Maine, to the south at least, massive overdevelopment of shorelines, the waterways overcrowded with fast powerboats too often operated by people with inadequate competence and basic courtesy, and, to me, a repelling degree of commercialization of many segments of the sport of sailing represent such a change from when I used to enjoy venturing south that I am happy to confine on-the-water time mostly to Maine. Both ocean sailing and cruising the whole eastern Caribbean were much enjoyed times afloat, but the changing character of ever more developed and crowded destinations, as well as increased difficulty finding friends and family members with adequate time, physical vigor, and the interest in offshore sailing to help crew, eventually led to reducing my interest in sailing trips far afield.

New joy in sailing came with the serendipitous discovery of an immaculately restored Herreshoff Fish-class sloop for sale, a sistership to the one which my father so regretted selling. With all five grandsons in residence with us in early August 2014, we enthused at the arrival on her trailer of a Herreshoff Fish Boat named *Perch*, built in 1925, superbly restored in 2005 by the craftsmen at the shop of MP & G in Mystic, Connecticut, and impeccably maintained since. Within forty-eight hours Brooklin Boat Yard had her rigged, the bottom painted, and on a mooring in Center Harbor.

Perch was warmly welcomed into Center Harbor's lovely fleet of wooden boats. Famed wooden boat photographer and Brooklin neighbor Benjamin Mendlowitz and www.offcenterharbor.com videographer Steve Stone lost no time in scheduling photography sessions on Eggemoggin Reach. They put a spectacular video of us sailing *Perch* online, and Ben used a magnificent sunset shot as the cover photo for his *2016 Calendar of Wooden Boats*.

On the waters of Eggemoggin Reach and Jericho Bay on board this Herreshoff masterpiece I find both peace and inspiration and, perhaps more than anywhere else, a feeling of being truly alive. In a troubled world and contending with the inevitable ups and downs of one's own life and of the lives of family and friends, a person needs opportunity for personal rejuvenation and reinvigoration. For me that means the out-of-doors, nature's beauty, ocean waters, and both the aesthetic and the excitement of an able sailboat cleaving those waters.

In *Perch* too I have found for me the ultimate expression of visual art and craftsmanship. When I row away from her on a sunny day, I am entranced by the interplay of light and shadow on the lovely curves of her white hull and the gleaming of her varnished wood. With a boat of modest scale I hugely enjoy having returned to my younger days' roots in wooden boats and the genius in design and construction that such boats represent. The actual wood I examine with much deeper scrutiny and appreciation than in the past—the grain, the condition and defects, and the use of different species for different purposes. I have learned to understand the role of wood in carbon capture and storage, and as I feast my eyes on *Perch*, I fully appreciate the use of this wonderful material from nature that can be and should be managed sustainably. With *Perch* I feel more steward than owner, exactly as a landowner may feel about a parcel of land with outstanding natural attributes—indeed just as Dianna and I feel about the bird habitat on our Meadow Brook Farm.

Herreshoff Fish Boats and the Maine coastal landscape come together in providing me with a reassuring sense of constancy even in the face of large-scale change. A 1939 photograph of Center Harbor shows my father's Fish Boat in virtually the exact location where her sistership *Perch* now moors. The wheel indeed turns. Fascinating to see in that photo and proving that Maine has changed greatly, even if more slowly than most of our country, is the emptiness then of the now packed harbor, but the picture also demonstrates lack of change that I so value. Chatto Island forms the photograph's downeast background, spruce and fir towering above granite shores just as the same scene looks today, an example of the continuity of nature and beauty that has been such an underpinning of life for me and many others who cherish our coastline.

A few years ago that lovely Maine vista of Chatto Island and of other islands beyond was the focus of attention at an event hosted by Dianna and me for Maine Coast Heritage Trust friends. These were all people dedicated to helping preserve for as long as possible—with luck, forever—what makes the Maine landscape so special and important. The islands before us, most protected by conservation easements, showcase what dedicated conservationists already have achieved and are inspirational in encouraging continuation of well-planned and executed conservation efforts. The people who stood there that day gazing out over Eggemoggin Reach were, like us, parents and grandparents. They were thinking more about coming generations than themselves, considering not only how best to preserve Maine's extraordinary quality of place, but how to instill in the coming generations full understanding of what it means to enjoy and appreciate the outdoors and to conserve it. The future of Maine, the world, and even civilization depends on such shared passion and commitment being passed down.

INDEX